Doing the Impossible!

God Manifesting His Supernatural Power through You!

Part 1

Rudi Louw

Copyright © 2015 by Rudi Louw Publishing.

All rights reserved solely by the author. No part of this book may be reproduced in any form *without the permission of the author.*

Most Scripture quotations are taken from the RSV®, *Revised Standard Version*, Copyright © 1983 by Thomas Nelson, Inc.

Some Scripture quotations were taken from the NKJV, *New King James Version*, Copyright © 1983 by Thomas Nelson, Inc.

The Scripture quotations not taken from the RSV, and NKJV are a *literal translation* of the Scriptures.

The Holy Scriptures are just that, HOLY.

Statements enclosed in brackets were inserted into Scripture quotations to add emphasis or to clarify the meaning of what is being said in those scriptures.

The integrity of God's Word to man was not compromised in any way. Due care and diligence was cautiously exercised to keep the Word of Truth intact.

Table of Contents

The Marvel of the Holy Bible 5
Foreword 11
Acknowledgment 15
1. A Fresh Expectation! 19
2. Witnesses of and to God's Majesty! 27
3. Entering into the realm of the Supernatural 57
4. "Hail, o Favored One!" 69
5. Good News, Not Bad News! 85
6. The Gospel Came to Replace the Law 95
7. Fully Embrace The Gospel! 105
8. Agree with God! 115
About the Author 145

The Marvel of the Holy Bible

1. Uninterrupted Theme and Inspired Thought

It took *1,500 years* to compile the Holy Bible, involving *more than 40 different authors*. Yet the theme and inspired thought of Scripture continues *uninterrupted* from author to author, from beginning till end.

2. Absence of Mythical Stories

Compare philosophies and theories about creation in the Middle East, Europe, Asia, Africa, and Latin America and you'll find mythical scenarios: gods feuding and cutting up other gods to form the heavens and the earth, etc.

In ancient Greek mythology, the Greeks see Atlas carrying the earth on his shoulders. In India, Hindus believe eight elephants carry the earth on their backs.

But in contrast, Job, the oldest book in the Holy Bible, declares that, *"God suspends the earth on nothing."(Job 26:7)*

This was said millennia before Isaac Newton discovered the invisible laws of gravity that delicately balance every planet and sun in its individual circuit.

Contrary to every other ancient attempt to give a creation account, *the Holy Bible pictures the creation of the earth in a very scientific manner.*

For example, in Genesis Chapter One, the continents are lifted from the seas, then vegetation is formed and later animal life, all reproducing *'according to its own kind',* **thus recognizing the fixed genetic laws.** In addition, we have the bringing forth of man and woman, *all done by God in a dignified and proper manner, without mythological adornments.*

The balance or remainder of the Holy Bible follows suit.

The narratives are **true historical documents***, faithfully reflecting society and culture* **as history and archaeology would discover them thousands of years later. Not only is the Holy Bible historically accurate, it is also reliable when it deals with scientifically proven subjects.**

It was never intended to be a textbook on history, science, mathematics, or medicine. *However, when its writers touch on these subjects,* **they often state facts that** *scientific advancement would not reveal, or even consider, until thousands of years later.*

While many have doubted the accuracy of the Holy Bible, time and continued research have consistently demonstrated that the Word of God is better informed than its critics.

3. Intactness

Of all the ancient works of substantial size, *the Holy Bible survives intact, against all odds and expectations.*

Compared with other ancient writings, the Holy Bible has more manuscripts as evidence to support it than any ten pieces of classical literature combined!

The plays of William Shakespeare, for instance, were written about four hundred years ago, after the invention of the printing press. Many of his original writings and words have been lost in numerous sections, *yet the Holy Bible's uncanny preservation has weathered thousands of years of wars, contradictions, persecutions, fires and invasions.*

Through the centuries Jewish scribes have preserved the Holy Bible's Old Covenant text, **such as no other manuscripts have ever**

been preserved. They kept tabs on every letter, syllable, word and paragraph. They continued from generation to generation to appoint and train special groups of men within their culture **whose sole duty it was to preserve and transmit these documents <u>with perfect accuracy and fidelity</u>.**

Who ever bothered to count the letters, syllables, or words of Plato, Aristotle, or Seneca for that matter?

When it comes to the New Testament, the actual number of preserved manuscripts is so great that it becomes overwhelming. **There are more than 5,680 Greek manuscripts, more than 10,000 Latin Vulgate manuscripts and at least 9,300 other versions. Further still, there exists an additional 25,000 manuscript copies of portions of the New Testament.** **No other document of antiquity even begins to approach such numbers.**

The closest in comparison is Homer's <u>Iliad</u>, with only 643 manuscripts. The first complete work of Homer only dates back to the 13th century.

4. Unmatched Accuracy in Predictive Foretelling

The Holy Bible is unmatched in accuracy in predictive foretelling. .No other ancient

work succeeds in this, or even begins to attempt this.

Other books such as the Koran, the Book of Mormon, and parts of the Veda claim divine inspiration; *but none of these books contain predictive foretelling.*

This one undeniable fact we know for certain: *While microscopic scrutiny would show up the imperfections, blemishes, and defects of any work of man, <u>it magnifies the beauties and perfection of God</u>. Just as every flower displays in accurate detail the reflection and perfection of beauty, <u>so does the Word of Truth when it is scrutinized</u>.*

Historian Philip Schaff wrote:

"Without money and weapons, Jesus the Christ conquered more millions than Alexander, Caesar, Mohammad, and Napoleon. Without science and learning, He (Jesus the Christ) shed more light on things human and divine than all philosophers and scholars combined. Without the eloquence of schools, He (Jesus the Christ) spoke such words of life as was never spoken before or since and produced effects which lie beyond the reach of orator or poet. Without writing a single line, He (Jesus the Christ) set more pens in motion and furnished themes for more sermons, orations, discussions, learned volumes, works of art, and songs of praise

than the whole army of great men of ancient and modern times combined." (*The Person of Christ*, p33. 1913)

Today, there are literally billions of Bibles in more than 2,000 languages.

Isn't it about time you find out what it really has to say?

Hey listen, the Holy Bible is all about Jesus, the Messiah, the Christ…

…and everything about Jesus Christ is really about YOU!!

Study Tips:

Read 2 Corinthians 5:14, 16, 18, 19, and 21.

In the light of these Scriptures, it should be obvious that, if you want to study the Holy Bible, *you should study it in the light of Mankind's redemption!*

Feed daily on **redemption realities** found in the book of Acts, in Romans Chapters One through Eight, and in Ephesians, Colossians, and Galatians. These realities may also be found in 1 Peter Chapter One, 2 Peter Chapter One, James Chapter 1, as well as in 1 and 2 Corinthians.

Foreword

Thank you for taking the time to read this book.

Let me start off by saying that *I am totally addicted to my Daddy's love for me.*

I am in love with Jesus Christ, *and that is enough for me!*

The love of God is so much more than a doctrine, a philosophy, or a theory. It is so much more and goes so much deeper than knowledge; it way surpasses knowledge. *We are talking heart language here.*

I write *to impact people's hearts,* to make them see the mysteries that have been hidden in Father God's heart concerning Christ Jesus, and actually *concerning THEM,* so as to arrest their conscience with it, *that I may introduce them to their original design and to their true selves,* **and present them to themselves perfect in Christ Jesus** *and set them apart unto Him* **in love***,* as a chaste virgin.

We are involved with the biggest romance of the ages. Therefore this book cannot be read as you would a novel: *casually.* It is not a cleverly devised little myth or fable. **It contains revelation and** *truth* **into some things you may or may not have considered before.**

It is not blasphemy or error though. *It is the TRUTH of God, ultimate TRUTH, and therefore has direct bearing upon YOUR life.* **The Word and the Spirit are my witness** *to the reality of these things!*

Be like the people of Berea the apostle Paul ministered to in Acts 17:11. Open yourself up to study the revelation contained in this book *to discover for yourself the reality of these things*.

Be forewarned! Do not become guilty of the sins of the Pharisees, **or you too will miss out on the depth of fulfillment God Himself, who is LOVE, wants to give you**.

Jesus said of the Pharisees and Sadducees that they strain out every little gnat BUT swallow whole camels. What He meant by that is that *some people seem to have it all together when it comes to doctrine and they love to argue.* **It makes them feel important, but it is nothing other than EMPTY religious and intellectual pride.** *They know the Scriptures in and out, and YET they are still so IGNORANT about* **REAL TRUTH that is only found in LOVE.** *They are still so ignorant and indifferent* **towards the things that REALLY MATTER**. *They are always arguing over the use of every little jot and tittle and over the meaning and interpretation of every word of Scripture.*

The exact thing they accuse everyone else of doing though, the precise thing they judge everyone else for, *they are actually doing themselves.* That is **they often downright misinterpret and twist what is being said, making a big deal of insignificant things while obscuring or weakening God's real truth: the truth of His LOVE**. They are always majoring on minors **<u>because they do not understand the heart of God</u> and therefore they constantly miss the whole point of the message**.

Paul himself said it so beautifully,

*"…the letter kills but **the Spirit BRINGS LIFE**;"*

*"…<u>knowledge puffs up</u>, but **LOVE EDIFIES**."*

I say again:

*Allow yourself to get caught up in the revelation I am about to share. Open yourself up to study the insight contained in this book, not only with a desire to gain knowledge, but also with anticipation **to hear from Father God yourself**;*

…to encounter Him through His Word;

…and to embrace truth, in order to know and believe the LOVE God has for <u>you</u>, *so that you may get so caught up in it*, **that you too may receive from Him LOVES' impartation of LIFE.**

13

This revelation contains within it the voice and call of LOVE Himself to every human being on the face of this earth. *If you take heed to it, it is custom designed and guaranteed to forever alter and enrich your life!*

Acknowledgment

I want to acknowledge and thank one of my mentors in the faith, Francois du Toit, for blessing and impacting me with revelation knowledge.

I borrowed the portion on *"The Marvel of the Holy Bible"* from his website: http://www.MirrorWord.net, as students so often feel they have a right to do with things that come from teachers they respect. Just as Galatians 6:6 says, *"Let him who is taught the Word **share in all good things** with him who teaches."*

To all our dear friends and family, for all the love and support, and to Chase Aderhold and all those who helped me with this project:

THANK YOU!

Also, especially to my wife, Carmen;

For keeping me real by being my companion in life and partner in ministry,

I love and appreciate you so very much!

"You shall receive power when the Holy Spirit has come..."

"...and you shall be My witnesses...

...in Jerusalem, Judea, and all of Samaria

...and to the utter most parts of the earth."

— Acts 1:8

"Be not afraid; for behold, I bring you good news of great joy, which is to all people!"

"Glory to God in the highest, and on earth, peace, and good will towards all men, in whom God is well pleased!"

– Luke 2:10 & 14

Chapter 1

A Fresh Expectation!

It is so easy to pick up a book someone else has written, especially if you have some knowledge on the subject or have had some experiences of your own, and then to have a know-it-all-attitude and to shut your heart to receiving, while thinking to yourself,

'Well, I've had my own great experiences in God, and I have had my own mighty thrusts in my walk with Him. I've had great and mighty breakthroughs, and I've even had my own experiences where at times in my life I've been able to step out of the ordinary into the extraordinary, the supernatural, into that dimension of life and experience that I know God has prepared for me...'

But listen, as you read this book, I do not want you to rest in and be satisfied with yesterday's blessing. *I desire to stir you and quicken you, and get you to a place in your heart where you begin to develop a fresh anticipation of new exploits God wants to lead His whole "Church" into, you included!*

Listen, God wants to lead you and I as individuals, as well as corporately as the body of Christ in the earth, to new heights of experiences in Him and doing exploits in His mighty Name.

God wants us to begin to lay a hold of the impossible ...and no longer shrink back, or just sit there and be paralyzed, *weighing the counsel of this world as if there were gold in that counsel.*

God wants us to embrace His wisdom, instead, and begin to recognize that the counsel of this world is as refuse, in comparison with the counsel of the Holy Spirit of Truth: the *"Parakletos"* - the comforter; the confidence builder, the faith-builder, the One who has come to be with us and abide in us and live in us!

He has come to counsel us from within and instruct us in our spirit so that we may know and correctly discern because there is a way of doing things which seems right to a man and that way has to do with weighing different opinions ...but it is fruitless because the end thereof is death; the fruit of that way has no value, it is empty; *it has no real gain!*

God has ordained your life in order for you to gain the experience that He promised to every one of us, to profit from what He has promised and to gain that life; *the abundant life.* He's ordained your life in order for you *to come fully into that kind of an existence!*

But you see, while we live within the restrictions and the boundaries of the flesh; *living a mere ordinary life,* we begin to again behave **like mere men,** *like earth bound people;* like the ignorant masses, **when Jesus so clearly revealed and therefore birthed within us His own extraordinary nature!**

Through revelation knowledge Jesus birthed within us the ability to walk even as He walked.

Therefore the apostle John declares in 1 John 4:17 that, *"As He is,* **even so are we <u>in this world</u>***"*

So God wants us to invade and take over that realm of the impossible. It is our inheritance as sons of God! God wants us to learn how to operate in that other dimension, how to live in the spirit dimension, so we may experience the supernatural as a daily reality in our lives, and launch out into that realm of living that is above the ordinary; above the normal hum-drum of day-to-day living.

Whether you are a housewife, or a businessman, or involved in some sort of ministry or religious organization on a full time basis, God desires for you and I to live in the supernatural, to live in the extraordinary; *to live in the spirit-realm.*

He wants us to live in the realm of intimacy with Him, the realm of the miraculous, so that our lives will give testimony to the glory of the God **who is <u>love</u>** ...to the very glory of a supernatural God, **who is our <u>Daddy</u>**, the almighty creator of the universe, who upholds all things by His Word, by His gospel, **by the power of His love for us** ...so that we would not merely need to rely on and lean upon the plausible words of human excellence and human intelligence.

Listen, once we truly grasp what the gospel actually says and what it actually implies, we need not lean upon the cleverness of our arguments ever again. **We can lean hard upon the One who shows forth His power, upon the One who answers with power and demonstrates His love in practical ways, the One who confirms His gospel with signs and wonders and miracles and manifests Himself mightily through us in Spirit and power!**

God manifests and demonstrates Himself by the power of His Spirit, through our lives, as we give testimony to His glory! **We are called to be witnesses of and to His glory.**

Acts 1:8 makes it clear that God's call upon His *"Church",* His call upon us, the believers, His call upon His children, all of us, is to be His witnesses.

And so, if my life, no matter what office I occupy, no matter what particular function I operate in within the body of Christ, **if my life is not a witness, a distinct sound**, *that brings distinct and clear witness to the glory and the majesty of His triumph over the enemy, over the principalities and powers and rulers of the darkness of this age,* **then I have no witness at all!**

But hey, you don't have to simply take my word for it! Let's take a look at what Jesus said there in Acts 1:6-8,

"And when they had come together they asked Him, 'Lord, Will you at this time restore the kingdom to Israel?"

"He said to them, 'It is not for you to know times or season which the Father has fixed by His own authority.'"

Remember that the expectation of that age Jesus lived in, and so also the expectation of His disciples, was for a Messiah, a Redeemer like Moses who would again restore the kingdom of Israel, and make it become even a greater kingdom than in the days of Kings David and Solomon.

They were looking for the kingdom of God to be a natural kingdom, centered in Israel, in Jerusalem, from which God and His Messiah would exercise authority, ruling over all the surrounding nations, and perhaps even over all the other nations of the world; perhaps even Rome itself.

And so His disciples wanted to know from Him how and when He was going to set up that kingdom, but if they had only paid attention, and if they weren't so stubbornly clinging to their own preconceived ideas and expectations, they would have remembered that Jesus had already answered them earlier on, back in Luke 17:20-21 and other places, saying to them, and I paraphrase:

*"This kingdom you are seeking for is not a natural phenomenon; it's not a fleshly or natural kingdom. It has nothing to do with the restoration of Israel as an earthly kingdom again, to be reckoned with and respected globally by other nations! No, **the kingdom of the Messiah, the kingdom of God, is within you! It has everything to do with that which is already within you!**"*

But let's get back to Acts 1:7-8,

"He said to them, 'It is not for you to know times or season which the Father has fixed by His own authority.'"

He basically let them know in so many words that the nation of Israel's times and season *had already come and gone,* and that there was nothing that could be done about that now, **for the Father in His authority had His mind fixed on even greater things,** *'things I am trying to bring to your attention, even though you are being distracted with your mere* *natural-minded fleshly concerns! Listen, I know you would like to have your questions answered* **BUT there is something else of far greater significance I want to bring to your attention right now**...'

"'**BUT**...' *he says to them, pay attention, I want you rather to focus on this:* **'you shall receive power when the Holy Spirit has come...'**"

'...*you shall receive* **power**' (or **dunamis** in the Greek: **an enabling, an empowerment**)

'...*you shall receive* "**power**"

For what purpose?

For an enabling, an empowerment; the power to comprehend these things the Father has fixed by His own authority, things about the kingdom of God and its reality within you, which He has made His mind up about, things which belong to you already but you cannot grasp now!

"You shall receive revelation knowledge; you shall receive an enabling, and an empowerment by the Holy Spirit; the Spirit of Truth Himself,"

"...and you shall be My witnesses in Jerusalem, and in all of Judea, and all of Samaria, and to the very utter most remote parts; the very ends of the earth."

We might come back to Acts Chapter One later, but right now I want us to go take a look at Mark Chapter Nine.

Chapter 2

Witnesses of and to God's Majesty!

If you have your Bible, please go with me to Mark 9:17. I want to show you something there. (If you don't have your Bible with you, don't worry about it, just follow along.)

"One of the crowd answered Him and said: 'Teacher, I brought my son to You, for he has a dumb spirit;"

Notice that he brought his son to Jesus, but Jesus wasn't there. He was somewhere else, busy being transfigured before Peter, James and John, on the mountain. So, needless to say, this man was rather disappointed. He came to meet with Jesus. He came expecting to see Jesus in the midst of the crowd of disciples. When he recognized some of the disciples, he assumed that Jesus must be somewhere in that group, and usually whenever Jesus was around the supernatural was possible. Usually wherever Jesus was, the supernatural was present also.

So, just like countless others before him, who came to Jesus, and testified to this man of how

Jesus fixed their problem, he had now also come, hoping that he could bring his situation to Jesus and it could be dealt with, because He was the man of the hour, the mighty miracle worker!

But now this man was disappointed because Jesus was somewhere else. He was up on the mountain, in the glory of His Father. Jesus' natural body was transfigured before the very eyes of three of His closest disciples, supernaturally, by the power and majesty of God. The very brilliance of the sun was matched and began to pale in comparison; it was darkened in the face of the Son of God, when suddenly those disciples witnessed His majesty!

Peter wrote about this experience in 2 Peter 1:16, *"...we did not follow cleverly devised myths ...but,* **we were eyewitnesses of His majesty!***"*

Peter said, *"****We saw His majesty!****"*

They beheld the majesty of God transforming this man Jesus, transforming His natural body into the brilliance of the sun, into the very brilliance of light itself. It was and is a significant sign and revelation. It was a revelatory, insightful, and revolutionary message given to Peter, James, and John, and really to the whole world, through their witness, about the fact that *Moses and Elijah are not even in the same league as Jesus Christ, which is why Moses and Elijah disappeared out of sight* and Jesus was left standing there alone. Then on top of that, God's voice boomed out of heaven saying, *"This is my beloved Son in whom I am well pleased,* **listen to <u>Him</u>***!"*

Just in case you missed it, the revelation and message, to them and to us, was to listen to Jesus, instead of Moses, who represents the Law, and Elijah, representing the prophets of old. They were merely signposts and shadows, pointing to the coming of this Jesus, the Christ. In other words, they had incomplete revelation, BUT *"the substance is of Christ."* That means: **The sum total of revelation, the substance of truth, ultimate truth itself,** *is* **found and revealed in Christ.** - Colossians 2:17 (15-23)

So while all this was happening there on that mountain, unbeknown to them, something else was happening, something else was going on down there in the valley where the rest of the disciples were waiting, and arguing amongst themselves over which one of them was the greater, more spiritual, and therefore more deserving of recognition and honor among them.

They were self-absorbed in their vain and empty self-righteous pride, squabbling and arguing and fighting with one another.

And so it was, while they were still in the middle of their squabbles, that this desperate father approached them looking for help, looking for Jesus. Needless to say, the man was disappointed when, instead of Jesus, he found only Jesus' squabbling disciples. But he was desperate and so he approached them anyway, asking for help with his son who needed deliverance.

So while the transfiguration was happening and God was speaking so clearly on the mountain, there was, in stark contrast, a perhaps sincere, but ridiculous excuse for ministry, going on down there in the valley. It was a ministry of inferior intersession; a ministry of *"travailing."* They were *"fighting"* and *"battling"* with a deaf and dumb spirit, and attempting to cast that thing out. Those sincere ignorant pompous know-it-alls were trying their best to get rid of that spirit out of that man's precious little boy, *but nothing was happening.*

But, I thank God that, in the middle of their *"warfare"* and their *"struggling"* Jesus returns from the mountain, and the father, who was smart enough not to waste another minute with the dead religious efforts of those whose consciences were defiled by their own prideful arrogance, ignorance, guilt, shame, doubt, and unbelief, came running to Jesus and says to Him,

"Teacher, I came and I brought my son to you, for he has a dumb spirit. And wherever it suddenly seizes him, it dashes him down and he then foams and grinds his teeth and becomes rigid ...and I asked your disciples to cast it out, but they were not able."

In other words: *'I have an accusation and a complaint Jesus. You were not around, so I asked Your disciples to do it. You were somewhere else and I resent You for that, I resent you for not caring enough to be here when I needed You. I don't know what You were doing exactly way up on that mountain that was so important. My point is: You were not around; You were somewhere else. But in Your absence, I asked Your disciples for help, and Your disciples failed me!'*

Can you just hear the world's frustration today?

*'Where is Jesus? If we can just have the real Jesus around today ...but He's gone somewhere else. He's in glory with His Father! And so we've asked His disciples but they cannot help us! Somehow they just do not have what Jesus walked in! Somehow they just fail to communicate and minister **the very power and demonstration of Gods glory** as Jesus did!'*

But in case you wonder what Jesus would say to all this, you need not wonder. I mean we need not go and try to figure it out for ourselves. It is actually recorded in the Scriptures in black and white, and in some cases even in a special red letter addition!

Ha... Ha... Ha...

Hallelujah! I thank God for the Scriptures!

All we need to do is look to see what Jesus has to say here in Mark 9:19,

"And Jesus answered him..."

Now notice Jesus' response. Jesus wasn't defensive, nor insensitive, **but in His compassion He was very direct.**

He didn't say to the man, *'Sorry dude, you came at the wrong time. You should have waited for me. If I'm around I can do it, so you should have waited for ME. I mean, don't expect things like that from My disciples. They're not equipped to do that!'* NO! **Jesus speaks very directly and He answers us all,**

He says,

"Oh generation without faith *(faithless* means: to be without faith; *to be without proper understanding)..."*

You see, Jesus didn't tell them, *'Well, maybe you just didn't pray long enough or hard enough. Or maybe you just didn't say the right words, or maybe you forgot the right formula, maybe you forgot to fast, maybe you just failed in that specific area...'*

NO! He said, *'Oh generation without faith'* In other words, *'You have a faith problem. You are busy with your own attempts at faith. You are busy with your own faith; **you are not busy with the faith of God!**'*

He said: *"How long am I to bear with you?"*

It means: *"How long will it take for you to get these things?"*

"How long am I to bear with you?"

Mark 9:19,

"Oh generation without faith, how long have I to be with you? How long am I to bear with you? Bring him to Me."

"And they brought the boy to him; and when the spirit saw Him..."

I want you to see that spirit recognizes spirit. You cannot deceive a spirit. That spirit will deceive *you,* but *you* cannot lie to *it*. It will lie to you, because it is of its father, the devil.

Spirit recognizes spirit.

Remember when those guys in Acts 19 wanted to cast out a devil in the name of the Jesus ...not whom they truly believed in, but whom

Paul preached? And that devil said, *'Huh? Listen, Jesus we know, and Paul we know, but who are you?!'* And the person they were trying to deliver overwhelmed them and beat them up, and ripped off their clothes, and they were forced to escape and run for their lives away from that spirit inside that man. They ran away naked and embarrassed, and others saw them running down the street, and laughed at them!

"...Jesus we know, and Paul we know, but who are you?!"

So spirit recognizes spirit.

Back to Mark 9:20,

*"And they brought the boy to him **and when the spirit saw Him**, immediately **it** convulsed the boy, and he fell to the ground and rolled around, foaming at the mouth."*

I want you to know that this experience is supernatural. It is not just a natural thing occurring. It might have a natural connection, a natural tie, or a natural origin, but it might not. It might even be both natural and supernatural, *but I want you to know that this whole experience described here is not just natural, **it is supernatural!***

It is not natural for a little boy to suddenly, for no apparent reason, fall and roll around on the ground and do strange things!

I know normal little boys are known to throw tantrums at times and that needs to be addressed by their parents to get them to mature out of that habit, but here in this scenario is a little boy who suddenly just acts totally unnatural. Something seizes him and violently throws him to the ground and he starts to foam at the mouth.

Now that may sound like a normal seizure condition or disorder, but I want you to notice that His parents began to look at this child of theirs and they recognized that there was a different presence in this child. They recognized that this child was not like all their other children, or the other children of their little village.

There was something, another presence, another being, within this child of theirs, that was stronger than the child, *stronger than the child's father even!*

And his father, who knew him well, would recognize that the child was not himself and that there was a different presence that suddenly seized him. His personality would suddenly change, and he would start to foam at the mouth and this thing then suddenly, against his own will even, would throw him to the ground. It would suddenly just, without any warning, grab this child, and rip through his body, and throw him to the ground, and roll him around.

And this is what was so strange about it, *it would try to roll him into water and drown him, and sometimes into fire also, seeking to destroy him.*

You see the devil was trying, through this child's spirit, to demonstrate his own nature, to put his own nature on the platform, to show the human race what he is really like when the disguise is stripped off his face. He was trying to show Mankind that he is a thief and that he has come to steal, to destroy, and to kill. He was making himself know, and he was making his presence known, *trying to intimidate;* **trying to instill fear!**

And even today still, so many are trapped in his snare, and whatever innocence their sin which they are involved in might be wrapped and disguised in, **it is a poison that seeks to destroy them.**

And that devil, that sin, that poison distorts and convulses their whole being, and tries to rip them off, and destroy them, dragging them into hell. Many, many people are trapped in this kind of hell. It's a hell of their own making.

The devil, with their cooperation, knowing or unknowing, *through their creative imagination,* manipulates them, and works in and through them.

And so, this devil had this little stage that he used to intimidate the people and show them that their medicine and their psychiatry could not help this child. He was bound by an evil spirit. Perhaps that devil found opportunity somewhere to have access to his spirit and it controlled him. That spirit controlled his mind, and his actions, and this little boy had no one that was able to help him. And so his father brought his little boy to Jesus.

And in Jesus' absence the disciples *"battled"* with it and *"wrestled"* with it and tried to get rid of the spirit, but they failed. Perhaps it was partially because of the arguing they were just engaged in, which they knew Jesus wouldn't approve of, and it left them with a defiled conscience full of guilt and shame, feeling nonspiritual and disqualified. Either way, they didn't feel qualified; they didn't feel righteous and they had no leg to stand on. They had nothing left, no faith, and no confidence. They were full of their own doubts and unbelief, and therefore they failed.

Then they brought the little boy to Jesus, verse 21, *"And Jesus asked the father, 'How long has he had this?' and he said, 'From childhood. And **it** has **often** cast him into fire, and into water, to destroy him...'*

It is amazing how, for whatever period of time the enemy has access to someone's life, *how he builds up a historic reference.* Every one of us has a certain history to our lives, giving testimony to the sway and control which the devil has had. Sometimes that history itself can become a stronghold within our thinking, making the problem seem insurmountably big, like the size of Mount Everest, in our hearts and minds, and it affects our faith.

And so the father of this boy continues and he speaks from that reference and he says,

*"...it has **often** cast him into fire, and into water, to destroy him; **but if you can even do anything,** have pity on us and help us."*

He heard that this Jesus could do anything, but now he was not so sure about that anymore, especially in light of the severity and scope of this massive and serious problem, that had been persisting for so very long already. And especially now after the disciples themselves had also failed in making this problem go away!

He heard that the impossible was possible with Jesus, *"**BUT** Jesus, **if you can do anything**..."*

*'I mean, maybe this is too big of a problem, maybe the devil is just too strong, **even for you** Jesus...'*

*"but **if you can perhaps** do it, please have pity on us and help us!"*

Notice how Jesus challenged this man's doubts and his unbelief.

He said to the man, in Verse 23,

*"**If** you can!"*

*"What do you mean, '**If** you can!'?"*

Listen; *"**IF**"* **is one of the greatest enemies of faith!**

You see, just like so many other people, even in our day, *"**If** you can!"* was this man's kind of religious approach.

But Jesus, in essence, was saying to this man, *as well as to us, "Listen, stop your religious approach man. We are dealing with a real devil in this child! Father God, the God who is love, the One who cares deeply for this child, wants him delivered! Don't come with unbelief now! Now is not the time to come to Me with your unbelief! Listen man, don't come and approach this situation with your doubts, with a, 'Well, let's see' attitude!"*

*"It's because you came with that attitude that it isn't working for you! You see, that "**IF**" in your attitude dominated the whole ministry that was going on up to now!"*

*"But now that I am here I am not going to put up with that "**IF**", not from you, and certainly not from my disciples, or from anyone else ever, when it comes to helping a little child like this one or anyone else who is hurting and being tormented and in need, because Father*

God, their Daddy wants them free; He wants them whole!"

*"Hey man, my dear precious fellow, I know you are frustrated and hurting and full of fears and doubts, and you came to My disciples and you asked them, 'Do you think that, **perhaps**, Jesus could do it? But I can see He's not around, so do you think that, **perhaps**, you can do it ...**if** it's possible? ...**if** it's even possible!'*

*'...**and your whole approach has been wrong up to this point; your whole point of departure is doubt!**'*

*'...And I'm not just speaking to you right now, I'm speaking to everyone of my disciples now as well: '**Your whole point of departure is doubt, not faith, <u>that is exactly the reason why you failed to obtain what you where trying to accomplish!</u>**'*

Listen, Jesus didn't play around. In His love, in His compassion, He immediately addressed the seriousness of the issue at hand. I want you to know that he didn't just overlook their unbelief and doubt and went ahead and just dealt with that devil. NO! He first addressed them all and challenged their doubt and unbelief. He didn't even let the boy's father off the hook! He didn't just address his disciples and spare the man's feelings. No, in His love, in His compassion, He confronted and challenged His disciples as well as the father of the boy. **Because when it comes to faith and seeing results, there are no shortcuts.**

We must deal with our doubt and unbelief. It cannot be allowed to dominate and reign in our hearts**!**

*"What do you mean, '****IF*** *you can!'? Let Me both challenge you and encourage you at the same time with these words: **All things are possible to him*** *****who believes*****!"***

Listen, this is perhaps **one of the greatest statements in the Bible!** I have read many little commentaries where people try to compromise and undermine that statement of Jesus, and so they write and they say, *'Well, we can't really say **that**, you know. That's a bit bold, you know, that says a bit much.'*

And yes, I agree, *it says much!*

That is precisely why I want you to observe and know that Jesus committed Himself *to the kind of faith* **that pleases the Father,** *the kind of faith* **that breaks forth into the supernatural,** *that invades that realm of the unseen* **and enters in and occupies that realm,** *the realm of the impossible.* Listen, Jesus committed Himself, and also required of His disciples, as well as of us, *to be committed to* **the only kind of faith** *that pleases the Father.* **It's the very faith of God,** *on display in the Scriptures, in the life of Jesus,* *****in the very work of redemption, and in the gospel*****!**

Only insight into these things, *into that realm of the spirit* ...only an accurate understanding of these things, *of the knowledge of God* ...only a full revelation into the eternal truth of God, *a full persuasion in the truth of the gospel* ...only a full persuasion in these things, *in the very faith of God,* **can make possible the impossible!**

Listen, the faith of God is so much more than our own willpower. It's so much more than our own positive vibes and positive attitude and positive confession!

Listen, faith is not witchcraft! Faith is not like a magical Harry Potter wand you can just wave and say a few magical words, *and if you got the formula just right then you can make all your problems disappear!* Faith is not trying to somehow twist God's arm, *to get Him to obey your will!* No, faith is *knowing His will!* Faith can only operate through an intimate knowing of His will, of what *He deeply desires!* It can only operate based on that genuine and accurate knowing of *His eternal desire and will!*

When Jesus says, *"All things are possible to him who believes,"* we are not talking our own faith here, working ourselves up into an emotional tizzy and trying to convince ourselves of something, or just desperately trying our best to BELIEVE: *'It's gonna happen ...it's gonna happen ...it's gonna happen!'*

Faith is not of ourselves! It is not our own invention! The faith of God is not our own invention! The faith of God is a gift given to us all! Faith came in Jesus Christ. Paul talks about that fact in Galatians 3:25, and he says,

"Now that faith has come..."

You see, Jesus is the exact representation of the invisible God! He said, *"If you've seen Me, you've seen the Father."* Jesus is the will of the Father manifested! He is the intimate desire of God on display! He is the very heart of the Father revealed and made known!

Faith is the will of God revealed. It's the intimate desire of God revealed!

John says in 1 John 1 that all this *...that which was from the beginning, hidden in the heart of God,* **has been revealed and made known.** We refer to it as the Word of life. ***Jesus is*** *the Word of life* ***made flesh***.

John goes on to say that the purpose of revealing all this and making it all known, *the very purpose of the Word of life is* ***so that we may have fellowship with the Father and with His Son Jesus Christ!***

You see, **Jesus** *is both the alpha and omega.* ***He*** *is the very beginning and end of faith.* **True faith is sourced in Him!** And so, that Person revealed in Him, that faith revealed in Him, ***who He is****, is the same* (it is unchanging; ***He is***

unchanging), yesterday today and forever! Thus, **the very faith of God** *is eternally defined and put on display in Him!*

He wants us to have an intimate trust relationship with Him *based on that knowledge,* **based on that faith of God revealed!** He wants that intimate trust relationship, based on the faith of God revealed, *to then also* **produce faith in us!** Thus it is called *the faith of God!* Our faith is **inspired;** it is **produced** *by God Himself!* **Our faith comes *directly from God Himself!***

If faith is so clearly defined and sourced there, *in Him,* in Jesus, **why look anywhere else for it, *but Him?!***

I say again: **If the faith of God was indeed defined in Jesus and if that faith is then also sourced in Him, *then why try and define or obtain faith somewhere else?!***

Faith is sourced in God! *Faith is a living, relational thing! Faith is directly connected to* **trust!** Faith and trust go hand in hand! Thus *faith is the direct* **fruit** of **genuinely, intimately knowing God.**

Jesus said: *"I am the true vine* (the true source), *and My Father is the caretaker of the vineyard. Every branch of mine* (which is us) *that bears no fruit, He helps them. He lifts them up off of the ground and inspires them* (He changes their perspective, He moves them away from earthly thinking and He lifts up their countenance), *and every branch that does bear fruit he cuts to the heart, with revelation knowledge, with truth, so that they may bear more fruit. Listen, you are already made clean* (pruned) *by the word which I have spoken to you! Abide in Me, and I in you. As the branch cannot bear fruit by itself unless it abides in the vine, neither can you unless you abide in Me. I am the vine, you are the branches. He who abides in me, and I in him, he it is that bears much fruit, for apart from Me you can do nothing. If you abide in Me, and My words abide in you, you will ask whatever is inspired or quickened within you as a desire, and it shall be done for you!"* - John 15:1-7

Paul says in Philippians 2:13,

"For God is at work in us, both to will and to do of His good pleasure!"

He goes on to explain how this process works. **He talks about a living relationship with God, based on His word of truth, His gospel, abiding in us.** He puts it this way, he says, *"...holding fast the word of life!"* - verse 16.

Listen get this down on the inside of you: In Jesus, God our Maker, our Origin, ***revealed His deepest desires.*** **He revealed His will! He revealed that He wants relationship with us. He wants an intimate relationship;**

reconciliation ...*a genuine faith and trust relationship.* **He revealed that He wants the Fall that happened in Adam** *completely reversed!*

In Jesus, God our Father, our true Daddy **revealed that** *He wants us free!* **He desires freedom for us!**

In Jesus, God our Father, our true Daddy **revealed that** *He wants us healed!* **He desires it for us!**

In Jesus, God our Father, our true Daddy **revealed that** *He not only loves us and cares about us,* more than all of creation put together, **but He reveals that** *He is indeed <u>in love with us</u>!*

You see; **Jesus is indeed the will of God, the desire of God for us,** *revealed.* **Jesus is the heart of God towards us on display,** *the very faith of God defined and revealed!*

The truth of the gospel, the truth about us, the truth about the Father revealed in Jesus, the truth about His will, the truth about His heart towards us, about who He is and who we are to Him, about the work of redemption **as God sees it and knows it,** *is what constitutes the very faith of God!*

That is the only kind of faith Jesus wants us to occupy our hearts and minds with, *committing ourselves to it,* because it's the *only kind of faith that can make the impossible possible!*

"All things are possible to Him who believes!"

Focusing *on His initiative* in His love for us **quickens faith!** - Galatians 5:6

"We love Him, and we trust Him, ***because He first loved us!****"* - 1 John 4:19

Our faith is sourced *in His love!*

"It is not that we loved God, but that ***He first loved us!****"* - 1 John 4:10.

His love is the fuel of our faith! That is where faith comes from! That's where it originates, where it is rooted!

To be rooted and grounded in the love of God, **in what God believes and declares about you as revealed in the incarnation, in Jesus, and in the work of redemption** *is such a sure place to live from!*

The invisible God, our Maker, our Origin, our Daddy, the Giver of life Himself, the One who sustains all life, the very One who gives to all men, life, breath, and all other things, stepped out of eternity into time, and partook of our humanity. He took on flesh and became a man, **to reveal Himself, to make Himself known!**

*"We know that the Son of God has come **and has given us understanding, so that we may know Him <u>who is true</u>**, and we are in Him who is true ...**this is indeed the true God;** this is that eternal life made manifest! **This Jesus is the true God revealed!** And we are revealed also, in His Son Jesus Christ ...we are revealed to be in Him who is true ...**in His heart!**"* - 1 John 5:20

And now Paul says that, *"He who did not spare His own Self, but delivered Himself up to us all, how will He ...how will this God, our Daddy, who gave Himself to us in all His fullness, **not also give us all other things!**"* - Romans 8:32

But so often, whether it is educated man, or ordinary man, it seems that both groups are addicted to the same soul realm unbelief according to 1 Corinthians 1:22, *instead of embracing what God Himself has revealed about Himself and about us in Jesus!*

Listen, the educated intellectuals may revel in much philosophical debate, soul realm reasoning, but they rob themselves of faith!

And quite often the rest of us are no different. So often we crave signs to speak to our unbelief, *to calm our doubts.*

But faith comes when the truth of the gospel is embraced independently of soul-realm reasoning and soul-realm reality.

"Lay aside every weight, every yoke, every burden, and the sin of unbelief that so easily besets you! **Looking away unto Jesus, the author and finisher of faith!***"* - Hebrews 12:1 & 2

Faith supersedes soul-realm living! Faith does not measure the soul-realm! Faith does not originate from, nor operate, *on a mere soulish realm!* Faith does not therefore measure itself against the soul-realm! Faith does not measure and compete with soul realm!

Faith grasps and comprehends, it understands that **everything in the natural *is being upheld in the supernatural,* by God Himself,** by Him who does exist, yet cannot be seen by the natural eye!

"We live by faith, and not by sight!" - 2 Corinthians 5:7

God upholds all things by the word of His power. What is the word of His power? The gospel is the power of God! The power of God is directly linked to that Word! Faith is directly linked to that Word! Faith comes to us by the hearing of that Word, by the hearing of Christ, the hearing of the gospel clearly defined and made known! The gospel is the word of His power that upholds all things, *even faith!*

God's power is behind the gospel. He backs up that word with His power! He

upholds and enforces that word with His power!

The whole universe exists and is held together by the very message of the gospel, by the very love of God for us revealed in the gospel, and therefore it is held together by His power also!

If nothing can separate us from the love of God for us, as revealed in Jesus Christ, *then nothing can separate us from His power either!*

The gospel is the power of God unto salvation from anything! That is what faith is all about!

Faith is about *knowing and believing the Love God has for us!*

God is love, *and therefore, it is* **who God is** *that gives faith* **its ground to operate from!**

I say again: **It is LOVE, the very love of God for us, that gives faith its ground to operate from.** - Galatians 5:6

"All things are possible to him who believes."

All things are possible to him who believes and trusts in the love and power of God!

All things are possible to him who becomes persuaded in these realities!

Jesus once said to the Pharisees,

"You are in error, and go into error; you fail to succeed because you do not know these things as revealed in the Scriptures."

In other words: *"When you fail to succeed it is because you do not know the gospel, you do not believe the gospel. You do not believe in the gospel nor the power of God!"* - Mark 12:24

Mark 9:23,

And Jesus said to the man, *"What do you mean, 'IF you can!'?"*

*"Listen: **All things are possible <u>to him who believes</u>!**"*

"And immediately the father of the child cried out saying, 'I believe; help my unbelief...'"

A better translation would read,

"And immediately the father of the child cried out saying, 'I now believe! Forgive my unbelief!'"

Another way of looking at it is him saying, *"I do believe with all I've got! Help me, please. Help me anyway. My faith is still so weak and inferior, I am still so full of fear and it's making me doubt! I don't know what to believe in anymore. I am full of unbelief, please help me anyway!"*

I still prefer the first statement, *"I now believe, forgive me for doubting!"*

He cried out: **I do believe!**

That's the best thing that father did for his son that whole morning!

Either way, there was enough of an attitude change in that boy's father for Jesus to go ahead and take care of the problem with the boy.

Verse 25,

"And when Jesus saw that a crowd came running together (He refused to give that devil another audience to try and make an impression upon), *he rebuked the unclean spirit, saying to it, 'You dumb and deaf spirit, I command you, come out of him, and never enter him again.'"*

"And after crying out and convulsing him terribly, it came out, and the boy was like a corpse; so that most of them said, 'He is dead.'"

"But Jesus took him by the hand and lifted him up, and he arose."

Now here in Mark it is not very clear, but in Matthew's account of this same event, in Matthew 17:20 it says,

"And when He had entered the house, his disciples asked him privately, 'Why could we not cast it out?' And He said to them, 'Because of your unbelief!'"

Other translations say:

"Because of your little faith."

"Because of the littleness of your faith."

"Because you don't have enough faith."

"Because you have so little faith."

"Because your faith is so small."

"Because you were faithless (without faith)."

"Because of your lack of faith."

"It is through your want of faith."

But I like the ones that say, *"because of your unbelief."* In fact most translations say, *"Because of your unbelief!"*

He was referring to the natural-mindedness of that generation. Because religion had messed them up in their thinking when it came to their interaction with that unseen realm from which they came. **They did not know how to properly interact with that realm. They did not know or understand their authority in that realm.** They did not even know how to really even connect with God. Religion had messed them up in their heads, and so, *all they were left with was life in the flesh* **as mere men, as natural-oriented men only,** *and that's why they were filed with unbelief.*

Now some later manuscripts include another verse there, *but it was added on later and cannot be found in the older, original manuscripts.* That added on verse goes on to say in Matthew 17:21,

"But this kind never comes out except by prayer and fasting."

That story does conclude in Mark 9:29 with,

"And He said to them, 'This kind cannot be driven out by anything but prayer." But there in Mark it says nothing about fasting.

Another interesting thing to note is that the word, *"generation"* previously used and this word, *"kind"* used in this added on verse is the same word. Could it be perhaps that Jesus meant to say that this kind, this generation's unbelief you have inherited and passed down from your forefathers under religion does not come out except through talking to God and getting some real revelation imparted to you by the Spirit of God, by the Spirit of Truth Himself?

Now I don't know about you, but I have heard a lot of teaching on the subject of entering the realm of the supernatural. There are many of these kinds of teachings out there that claim that if you want to enter the realm of the supernatural and into the realm of deliverance, you need to fast a lot. Yet, when you go look at the older, original manuscripts from the Greek, there is no mention of fasting in this passage. And yet, this exact passage is the passage that most of these teachers use as their reference and foundation for their teachings.

I was surprised to find when I read in some of the commentaries on this passage, that that extra verse was added later on, when a resurgence of the old Pharisaical teaching and practice of fasting, an inherited practice of the old world steeped in mythology and witchcraft, became more and more of an accepted practice again in the Christian Church.

But I want us to go to Galatians Chapter Three to study what Paul had to say on these matters, because there in Galatians Paul taught on, and he made it so clear and so simple when he writes on *how to enter into the realm of the supernatural.*

Chapter 3

Entering into the realm of the Supernatural

Galatians 3:2,

"Let me ask you this..." says Paul,

"Did you receive the Spirit by the works of the law?"

*"...**Or was it the hearing with faith?**"*

*"Are you so foolish, having begun in the Spirit, **are you now ending up again in the flesh?**"*

*"**Have you experienced so many things** in vain? If it was really in vain"*

You see, these people had already encountered God and they had experienced the miraculous. They had witnessed the supernatural. But then Paul discovered that somehow a shrinking back from faith began to rob from the church in Galatia its life of the supernatural. And they were left with having to try and compliment their once powerful ministry with the efforts of the flesh again, which is inspired by and operates under the law; under religion.

You see, this is how the law works: If I fast *so long,* or if I intercede *so long,* or if I do this or that *enough,* **then eventually I gain enough merit,** so that I can **have enough approval** from the throne room, ***and then*** *God could be justified in blessing me with the supernatural.*

And so we find that somehow the church here in Galatia began to drift into this kind of thinking, this kind of condition, *where they were no longer living in a vibrant faith.*

They were no longer living in the full persuasion of the truth of the gospel, in the full persuasion of the integrity of the God who is love, so clearly put on display in Jesus and in the resurrection, and thus revealed and made known in the gospel ...and so they began to think and act like the Pharisees of old did, *trying to patch the old garment with some fasting again.*

Fasting under the Old Covenant played exactly that kind of role, for back then, immediately when you begin to discern that there was a slackness in your devotion, and you begin to discern perhaps that *you were not performing like you should in pleasing God,* then you would have no confidence before God. But you knew that at least, *if you were to fast and get this body of yours under your full control, then somehow you would also begin to experience some kind of a breakthrough in your spirit, some kind of boost in your confidence again,* that would lead then also perhaps to some kind of a spiritual breakthrough.

And so we can read how the Pharisees, as well as the disciples of John, came and approached Jesus in criticism, jealousy and resentment, wanting to know, *'Why is it that your disciples don't fast?'*

'Why is it that we all feel the need to fast, and yet you and your disciples don't see the importance and significance of it!'

'You somehow don't ascribe any importance to it! Why is it that You teach your disciples not to fast? Why is it that Your disciples don't fast?'

And listen now, don't get all defensive on me. I am not entirely against fasting. There are some medical benefits to it and there might still be some place for it spiritually. It might perhaps still be of benefit if you want to get alone just so you can spend some time with God in contemplation and intimate fellowship without the many distractions and demands of regular life. *Sometimes the Holy Spirit might even call you away to do just that,* <u>and then you can choose to fast some</u>.

But I am telling you now, **it's not a have to** *and I don't see the need for it myself.*

Jesus fasted so we don't have to!

It's not a have to, *especially for those who truly know who they are in Christ.*

There are other, better ways of getting connected with the Spirit and getting intimate with God, *without employing a fast.*

All we really need to do to be renewed in the spirit is to embrace afresh the truth of the gospel again.

We engage God, we interact and connect with the Spirit of God within us *through the abiding Word!*

So I still fast from time to time when being led by the Holy Spirit, *but I seldom do.* Most of the time when I do decide to go on a fast, I do it not so much for spiritual reasons, *but for natural reasons. You see, there are so many wrong concepts that have crept into the traditions of men,* **and especially when it comes to this subject of fasting,** *there is a seriously wrong concept that tradition has added to fasting* **and so we have missed it in our fasting and we have totally missed the reality of what God has in mind!**

So, spiritually speaking, *traditionally fasting was used as a little tread, as a little tug,* **to try and pull one back into spirituality again.** It was used *to try and raise the level of devotion again* and to try and patch up the old garment again that had perhaps developed a little tear or something. *So it was used to patch up one's garment of righteousness and raise their level of awareness of God and of His Spirit, as well as their level of devotion again.*

And so the Pharisees, as well as John's disciples, fasted often, and they came and asked Jesus, *'Why is it that your disciples don't fast?'* And Jesus tried to tell them that *in light of the New Testament it was an outdated reality, an outdated practice,* although He knew they couldn't get it. So He said to them, *'How can they fast when the bridegroom is around?'*

He said, *'Those days will come,* **but not as long as the bridegroom is present!**'

The bridegroom is still present today, amen! Hallelujah!

Later on in the book of John it speaks of those days Jesus mentioned. It speaks of it in Chapters 14 and 16, when Jesus said, *'In a little while you will weep, and the world will laugh! But again then in a little while, then you will laugh again!'*

I want you to see that **that little while is over!** Amen, hallelujah! *That little while has come and gone!* That little while can be counted on the calendar as *a mere three days!*

Listen, we don't have to wait another two thousand or three thousand years for Jesus to come back *so that our joy can come back!*

"...in a little while you will laugh again ...and then never stop laughing!"

No one can take away our joy from us ever again, for all eternity!

It's absolutely a wrong religious mentality that has caused the church to give that kind of weeping and waiting on Jesus impression to the world. It is nothing but stupid religious thinking, the kind of mentality that, *'We are still waiting for Jesus to return, while the world is mocking us and laughing at us!'* As if Jesus never returned and we are all just sitting around in misery, waiting for the so-called *'second coming,'*

And so those same, sour and suspicious religious group of people are now thinking and saying to the world: *'You just wait and see, when the second coming of Jesus is upon us, then you will stop laughing because then we'll be that victorious bunch that the Bible prophesies about!'*

No, listen: we waited, and then we witnessed the return of Jesus. He was sent, and He came from the Father, and then He accomplished all that He did in His death, and so also in His priestly office, as our high priest, and then entered into the throne room with His own blood, there *securing an eternal redemption for us.* **He returned from that mission to show to this world the nail**

piercings, the marks in His hands. He showed Thomas His nail scarred hands, and He had him put his hand in His side, where the spear had pierced His side. **And when He did that** *it became a settled deal in the minds of the disciples, as well as in all reality,* that Jesus pleased the Father in the offering of Himself. **Jesus justified the nature of the Father in the offering of Himself, when He became our justification also,** *justifying our design.* **He justified the Father's design of the human being. When He did these things** *our joy became a settled deal!*

He returned from death and He came back, **to give us Himself** *in all His fullness.* **He gave us His very Spirit.**

He came to restore us to our original design: *Man and God reconciled, in relationship again, united once more, closer than ever, living life together in one body, absolutely united, one in spirit, inseparably joined, one spirit with Him.*

He came back in the resurrection, *to restore to us our joy!*

He says, *'I will not leave you as orphans, but I will come back in the resurrection and give you the gift of Myself. I will give you My Spirit; I will give you the Spirit of Truth. I will give you the Holy Spirit,* **so that where I am you may be also,** <u>**so that your joy may be full**</u>*!'*

He says, *'I will give you the Holy Spirit. That is My gift to you. It is to your advantage that I leave you in the flesh, for when I return in the resurrection **I will also return in Spirit form!**'*

*'So when I do return in Spirit form, **when the Spirit comes,** He will not just be with you any longer, no, **He will be in you! He will abide within you! He will dwell within your spirit,** and He will be a witness within you that I am the resurrected One, the all-powerful One, who has always loved you, and who loves you still, the One **who will never leave you** nor forsake you!'*

'He will not allow you to continue to feel like orphans, you know. He will not leave you saddened, or let you walk around with sad long faces any more, fasting in despair, and merely hoping that somehow, some day, there might be feedback form heaven again, praying for the so-called 'second coming' to hasten, praying that somehow God will quickly wrap up this deal on the world...'

No, no, no! But rather thank God for the reality of the New Testament! We have entered into the revelation of the effect of Jesus' resurrection, and His indwelling in us NOW!

I have written some more about this whole conversation in John 14, 15, 16, and 17 if you want to delve a little deeper into it, in my book: *"Living In Your Father's Embrace!"*

You see it's because of that resurrection that there is a root system to my joy! My joy is no longer rooted in the feeling-system, in what I can taste, see, touch, or feel in my emotions, in my soul, in this natural soul-ruled sense realm! No! My joy is now rooted in the truth! My joy is now rooted in the faith of God! My joy is now rooted in the eternal reality of the new creation, in the established reality that Jesus died and was raised **and I with Him** *to newness of life!*

Hallelujah!

So Jesus said to those guys, to the Pharisees and the disciples of John, *'Listen,* **while the bridegroom is with them, how can they fast?'** And then immediately after that conversation, and you can go and read it in every account of those events, immediately after that conversation He makes this statement and He says,

'How can you pour new wine into old wine skins? How can you patch up an old garment with a new patch!'

Listen, the Holy Spirit wants to show us what He was really saying. He wants us to understand fully what He was referring to, what He meant when He said those things! You see, fasting always accompanies tears in the old garment, in that inferior robe of righteousness of the Old Covenant, that weak robe of righteousness under the law, a substandard righteousness that was of the law and of my own making. Fasting always accompanies tears in that old garment.

To do a study of garments in the scriptures is fascinating and you can go and study the garments of righteousness and soon you'll discover that the enemy has left us naked in this world. The witness of Satan's reign in your life is nakedness, it's shame, and there is a tear in the garment of righteousness. The polluted garment that you use to try and cover the nakedness of your flesh is torn, and instead of covering that nakedness, that hole in your heart successfully, you begin to actually emphasize it, and people begin to see it and recognize that poverty stricken condition of your spirit!

So I begin to feel like somehow I need to patch this thing up, I need to begin to mend this tear in the garment of righteousness. So I think okay, here I go, I'll start making a greater effort. Let's patch up this tear in my garment. Let's fast, let's intercede, let's labor. And here I am, back into the works of the flesh again, trying to reestablish my righteousness, trying to build up some merit that God could record in my favor, *and then one day maybe bless me with some return on that investment!*

But hey, that is the wrong kind of righteousness we are busy with. That is the righteousness of the law, a righteousness of the flesh, a righteousness of works, a righteousness of our own making!

Listen, the righteousness that is a gift from God, the righteousness of faith, *doesn't think and speak and act that way!* The righteousness of faith **doesn't ignore the success of redemption!** *It doesn't carry on with the law!*

The righteousness of faith is given to me **as a gift,** *apart from the works of the law!* The righteousness of faith **does away with the law!** It doesn't carry on **as if Jesus never came,** *and dealt with the fall and all its side effects and consequences,* as my Savior!

The righteousness of faith does not ignore and overlook and undermine such a great salvation!

The righteousness of faith recognizes that I am under a whole different dispensation, a whole new dispensation.

I am not under law *but under grace!*

The righteousness of faith sees and recognizes and acknowledges *everything that grace reveals is already given to me from before time began!* It sees and recognizes and acknowledges *everything that grace then also accomplished and reestablished and restored and gave back to me again as a gift,* in Christ Jesus, in that work of redemption!

The righteousness of faith communicates and acts in line with **God's eternal love dream revealed in Christ Jesus!**

The righteousness of faith speaks and acts in line with, in agreement with, the successful work of redemption, *in which Christ restored us to everything we lost through the fall,* **everything contained in God's eternal love dream for us!**

Chapter 4

"Hail, o Favored One!"

While we are on this subject, let's quickly go and take a look at Luke Chapter One.

Here we have the Spirit of God coming to Mary, the soon to be mother of Jesus, through the angel Gabriel, and this is what He said in Verse 28:

"And he came to her and said, 'Hail, o favored one, the Lord is with you, (Blessed are you among women!)'"

It is interesting to note that the wording used here in the original Greek is found only one other place in all the Scriptures. Paul used it in Ephesians 1:6 when he said that we have been made, *"accepted in the beloved!"* Thus we have been shown the same favor as Mary, the mother of Jesus, who carried Jesus in her womb. We too have been made and singled out to be carriers of the Christ! The Christ-life has been conceived and given birth to in us! Therefore Christ, the desire of the nations, in us, is the hope of glory!

"And he came to her and said, 'Hail, o favored one, the Lord is with you!'"

It sounds very similar to the same greeting which Gideon was greeted with. Remember when the angel came to Gideon while he was beating out grain in the wine-press, hiding away, trying to protect what little bit he had from being taken also by the enemy? Do you remember the persecution they were under because of the reign of the Midianites over them as a people? While they were still living in that bondage; while Gideon was hiding in the wine-press, trapped in that fear, in that kind of a life and existence, the angel appeared to him and said, *'Hail, Gideon, you valiant warrior!'*

Now do you think God would have said words like that to Gideon if that man did not receive some kind of favor from God, deserved or not? I mean, God saw how scared that guy was in his heart, hiding in the wine-press, *but He came and He greeted him with faith!*

God greeted Gideon with favor when He greeted him with faith!

'Hail, Gideon, you valiant warrior! The Lord is with you!'

And now here in Luke 1:25, Mary experiences that same presence, the presence and love of the Lord that accompanies God's angels.

She experiences that same presence of the Lord in the form of an angel, that same favor, that same encounter with faith, that same faith filled greeting, and she begins to enter into a new dimension.

This righteousness of faith; the deceleration of favor, this faith greeting filled with the faith of God, as well as her faith response to it, her full embrace of it, is her first step into a new dimension, into a new encounter and a new experience!

Listen, the first step to entering into a new dimension is discovering the favor of God that rests upon your life!

If you are living under a cloud of condemnation and inferiority, under a cloud of shame and guilt and self-loathing, *you will never enter the dimension of the supernatural and abide there!*

Come into His favor, man, discover fully for yourself the truth of the gospel of Jesus Christ. Discover that the good news is God's heartbeat for this world, and He would say to this world:

"I GIVE YOU FAVOR! MY FAVOR IS TOWARDS YOU! I HAVE FAVORED YOU! YOU ARE BLESSED AND HIGHLY FAVORED!"

Remember how the angels came to announce the good news, to celebrate the coming of the Messiah, to celebrate the coming of Jesus into this world? Remember their greeting to those shepherds guarding their flock at night, who saw them? Let's look at that quickly.

Luke 2:10,

"And the Angel said to them, 'Be not afraid!'"

I want you to know that fear goes hand in hand with the works of the law! Fear goes hand in hand with a sin-consciousness! Fear has to do with thoughts of punishment! Fear is a tormenting spirit! Fear is a voice, a voice of the enemy! Fear is an accusing voice! Fear is the voice of the accuser of the brethren *and it will keep you out of that supernatural dimension.* **It will keep you out of God's supernatural dimension for your life!**

Fear will keep you linked to your daily problems and the press; or the pressure, *and the whine they produce in your spirit!*

Fear is **the voice of *religion.***

The Scriptures make it clear in 1 John 4:18 that fear has to do with the law. Fear has to do with punishment, and that fear is connected to torment.

But John goes on to say that **there is no fear in love!** *There is no room for fear and doubt and unbelief and torment there!* **There is no room for fear *in love!*** There is no room for fear *in the gospel!* **There is no fear in love.** *"But God's perfect love,"* says John, *"casts out every fear!"*

Let's read it there, 1 John 4:18,

*"There is no fear in love. But perfect love **drives out all fear!**"*

Let's get back to Luke 2:10,

"And the Angel said to them, 'Be not afraid; for behold I bring you good news of great joy which shall be to all the people...'"

Verse 13 & 14 reads,

"And suddenly there was with the angel a multitude of the heavenly host praising God and saying, 'Glory to God in the highest, and on earth, peace and good will towards all men ...with whom He is well pleased!'".

Again, it is funny how many later manuscripts left out that last part that says, *"...peace and good will towards all men ...with whom He is well pleased!"* They have translated it all kinds of ways to try and water it down. They are much more comfortable with some vague statement of peace on earth only towards men of good will. This is all due to the fact that the early church later f*ell back into the law.* And so for them that kind of a gospel that says that God is pleased with Mankind became again *just too good to be true,* so they butchered that statement and excluded and removed that phrase, *"...with whom God is well pleased"* out of the later manuscripts. However, all the older and more accurate manuscripts clearly still included that statement and still kept the whole good news announcement to the world intact!

Fear is a thief that comes to steal, kill, and destroy. It's a tormenting spirit that has to do with thoughts of punishment. It's a religious spirit and it comes to eat you up on the inside and devour any kind of confidence you might have in your spirit. It comes to destroy you and to defile your conscience!

I say again: Fear has to do with thoughts of punishment! Fear is the voice of religion! Fear is a religious spirit! Fear is a tormenting spirit!

Do you remember when you got up in the morning to go to school, but you didn't do your homework? It made you feel sick to your stomach, and suddenly you weren't all that keen to go to school that day, because that trepidation, that anxiety of repercussion, that fear of punishment made you feel sick. But there weren't exactly any symptoms that could make you stay behind and not have to go to school. Those sick feelings had to do with this very subtle fear that was building up inside of you. Why were you tormented? Because you feared the punishment!

But listen, we need to realize that **One died for all!**

We need to realize that **He faced our punishment!** That He dealt with our whole expectation of wrath or some kind of punishment from God! We need to realize that the chastisement that brought about **our cure** was upon Him! **That perfect display of His love for us,** *while we were at our worst,* **casts out all fear!**

So over and over again we find the angels coming again with the same approach, *"Do not be afraid! Do not feel condemned,* **you are a favored one!"**

Listen, come into His favor, man. Discover the true gospel, amen, *and embrace it fully!* Come into your sonship, enter into the embrace of your Father, *your Daddy!* He loves you, amen! He *truly* loves you! **He is love!** Amen!

Hallelujah!

If you want to take a step out of the natural into the supernatural, you need to begin here! You need to realize that your sins are not only forgiven, *they are obliterated!* You need to realize that the enemy *no longer has any dominion over you.* In fact, **he never really had,** and he never really will, *except for our own ignorance.* Listen, don't be ignorant any longer man, *don't be ignorant!*

Paul emphasizes that exact point in 1 Corinthians 12:1 when he says, *"Concerning that which is spiritual, or concerning spiritual things, brethren,* **don't be ignorant. I do not want you ignorant!"** He says, *"I do not wish for you to be ignorant, brethren, concerning these things!"*

Do you know why this world is so ignorant of spiritual things?

Because they feel so cleaver, so wise, where the flesh is concerned!

We have spent so much time educating and nursing the flesh! We've spent so much time trying to become brilliant in our own person in the flesh, *in our natural identity,* and yet we have totally neglected the spirit. Our own spirits were neglected even; *our spirit-identity, as well as the indwelling Spirit of God!*

Listen, God says do not be ignorant when it comes to spiritual things! God wants to introduce us into the realm of the spirit, where the Spirit is Lord, because where the Spirit is Lord, **there is freedom!**

God wants us to enter into the dominion of the Holy Spirit, where He establishes within us, and through us, the dominion of the Lordship of Jesus in the earth today, *so that the witness of who we are, that witness to **who we are,*** can be without any contradiction, amen!

You see God wants to lead you into a new realm of living! God wants to bring you out of the frustration of what you've been involved with all this time!

And so God wants to say to you in this book, *'Listen there is more. There is infinitely more available for you to freely enter into!'*

But first of all He wants you to be transformed by the renewing of your mind, *to change your way of thinking* **in order to embrace and experience His favor. He wants you to know and believe the love He has for you!** He wants you *to experience* the smile upon His face just for you! **He wants you to know and believe that the smile of God is upon your life! He smiles upon you with favor!**

And listen, I am not just saying all this because I want to psych you up emotionally and just try and make you feel good! No, when we are talking about the truth of the gospel we are not engaging in some kind of sales talk, trying to sell you something! No, I am speaking from the very integrity of the revelation of the gospel, the good news revealed in Jesus Christ by God Himself!

Listen, if you somehow inherited a million dollars, perhaps from a relative you didn't even know was your relative, and you didn't know about it, and yet somehow I've heard about it and know about it, *what kind of person would I be if I kept that news to myself?* What kind of person would I be if I keep that good news a secret? *What kind of person would you think me to be if I kept that news from you!?*

You see Paul, talking about his ministry and the preaching of the gospel says, *"I am not ashamed of the good news, it is my privilege to make it known!"* - Romans 1:16

He says, *"I owe it to the world!"* - 1 Corinthians 9:16-23.

Paul says, *"**The love of God constrains me,** not the fact that God is full of wrath and that He stands ready to judge and punish this world, no, **but the fact that He loves this world, that He does not count the world's trespasses against them! That's what echo within me and motivates me in all my endeavors!**"*

He says, *"I'm going to take advantage of that truth, I'm gonna take advantage of the knowledge I have, that knowledge, that truth that, **if One died for all, then all died!**"*

He says, *"I'm gonna take advantage of it! **I'm no longer going to consider any man from a human point of view!**"*

*"But I am going to consider them **in the light of the favor of God towards them,** in the light of what that favor **has accomplished for them** in Christ Jesus!"* - 2 Corinthians 5:14-21.

Luke 2:10, 13 & 14,

"Fear not! For behold I bring you good tidings of great joy which shall be to all the people..."

The angels announced, *"Peace on earth towards men!"* *"...peace and good will towards all men ...with whom He is well pleased!"*

They said **He is well pleased with all men; with all Mankind!**

That pleasure, that pleasing must not be based on men's conduct then, but upon *the content of God's own heart.* It must be based on a greater reality, *on the ultimate truth, on His design of us, on His opinion of us, on His love for us, on our identity as children of God,* **and nothing else!**

Paul himself said in Romans 5:1,

"Having been justified by the faith of God, **now we have peace with God** *through our Lord Jesus Christ!"*

He starts every one of his letters with the same greeting: **"I greet you, with grace and peace, from God the father, and our Lord Jesus Christ!"**

The gospel announces peace on earth, *from God the Father!* **Good will towards all men! God is well pleased with Man!**

This is God's own introduction of the gospel!

"Behold I bring you glad tidings of great joy, which shall be to all the people!"

This is not the message of the weeping prophet Jeremiah anymore, speaking, *"Woe to you o Israel! God is getting ready to judge you! God is ready to punish you, to let you experience hell here on earth. He is ready to take away every blessing from you!"*

No these are the angels of God, God Himself saying and announcing, *"**Behold I have good news for you! We bring you glad tidings of great joy for all people!**"*

Isaiah prophesied about this day. He saw it in the spirit, and he said, *"Behold, the people who dwelt in a land of deep darkness have seen a great light; upon them light has shone! And the Lord says that the joy of them will be greater than the joy of when the harvest abounds!"*

I want you to know that this gospel that has been announced to us by God Himself, this gospel which first began to be proclaimed by Jesus Himself, and later by Paul and the rest of the apostles, **this gospel is the absolute truth!** It is indeed **worthy of full embrace!**

And, once embraced, *it imparts to you and produces within you a joy that cannot be measured,* **a joy unspeakable and full of glory!**

The gospel doesn't impart and produce an inferior joy, a poverty stricken joy that somebody has to keep trying to psychologically crank up every few days, every Sunday. No it is an eternal joy, *every bit as steadfast and secure* **as the truth** *spoken into your spirit!*

That great joy is the fruit of the gospel that gets spoken into your spirit! *As the truth of the gospel gets imparted into your spirit,* **faith and joy get imparted with it!**

Listen, *"there is joy and peace in believing!"* - Romans 15:13

"This joy shall be **to all the people** *...it shall come* **to all the people!"**

The angels didn't say, *'This joy is just gonna touch a few here and there.'* No, it shall not just be for a few, but it will come and it will spread and it will be **to all the people!**

Isaiah saw this prophetically. He saw the joy that would be extended and would come **to all the people** *and cover the face of the whole earth.* He prophesied about it in Isaiah 35,

"Therefore the redeemed of the Lord shall return, and come with singing unto Zion, **and everlasting joy** *shall be upon their heads..."*

Isaiah saw a highway in the wilderness. And you know, we used to read it all wrong. I don't know how the translators could have missed it, but they did. Our old translations used to read, *"...and the unclean shall not pass upon it!"* So we thought that highway, that easy way, that smooth way, was just for the holy Joe's, and nobody else would get near it, or even come close to making it onto that road. But Verse One of Isaiah Thirty-Five already says, *"The wilderness and the dry land* **shall be glad**" He says, *"The desert* **shall rejoice** *and blossom!"*

Verse 8 says,

"...and a highway shall be there!"

You see, all of us can testify of times of wilderness experiences in our life. Some people's whole lives feel to them like a desert; like a wilderness experience, it's pathetic, and it's no joke!

Although, if it wasn't so pathetic, it would actually be quite laughable, if you really think about it!

But listen, I didn't write this book to make you feel bad by laughing at you. The truth is, all of us know the wilderness experience, the depression of living without the joy of the Lord. We all at one point or another had to somehow make due, and we had to just take to the bottle or have this little experience or that little encounter with whatever, to just find or make some good come out of living. But Isaiah prophesying *about the effects of the gospel* says here that *"even the wilderness and the dry land, or the desert,* **shall be made glad!**"

He says, *"the desert* **shall rejoice** *and blossom!"*

Verse 8 says, *"...and a highway shall be there"*

And he goes on to say, *"...and the unclean shall in no way be able to pass by it without seeing it, they will not be able to miss that highway, they will even stumble over it! That's how apparent it shall be to them, it shall be obvious, it shall stand out to them. In other words, they will not be able to ignore it or avoid it, it will be that obvious!* **They will see it, and they will be redeemed by it!***"*

He says, *"***They will see it, and it will be for them to walk on!***"*

Jesus didn't come for the healthy; He came for the sick, amen! That highway was meant for the unclean; *it was meant for them,* amen. It was meant for the sick and the infirmed, *for them to walk on,* **to ease their suffering, and lead them out of that suffering.** It was meant for them, *it is their salvation* amen! *It was meant for the lost,* **to help them find their way,** *it was meant for them;* **it is their salvation!**

It is called the holy way, not to exclude others from that way, but because it is the way *that makes holy.* That Hebrew word for holiness used there is used as a noun which included the action of the verb. Thus, it's called the highway of holiness, *not because you are excluded from it if you are not holy, but because it makes you holy,* **it makes you whole, it brings you home, it rescues you out of the desert!**

*"The desert shall bloom **and rejoice!**"*

What shall bring about that effect in the desert? I mean, what shall affect the desert so as to bring about that kind of response, those kinds of results?

In Isaiah 55 he goes on to say that,

*"God will saturate the desert, the soil of our hearts, with His word, with the truth of the gospel, with the joy of the gospel, **so that the whole environment of our inner being will change.**"*

He says that,

*"**In place of** the thorn shall come up the soft-to-the-touch fir tree. **In place of** the brier-patch shall come up the flowering myrtle!"*

Chapter 5

Good News, Not Bad News!

I want you to know that, *all of heaven,* there in Luke Chapter Two, *could not keep quiet any longer.* This message carried so much weight, there was so much truth invested in this message about the Son of God that was about to be born, *that the whole of heaven was ready to explode in confirmation of the truth of what was being said!* There was so much weight invested in these words of the gospel, i*n this good news announcement* **of the coming revelation of God in Jesus,** that a multitude of heavenly host *suddenly joined the angel who was sent with the message.* They had to glorify God! *They felt compelled to glorify Him* **because of the goodness of what was being declared and about to be revealed in this Jesus** who was being prophesied about!

You see we would expect the angels to say, *'Well boys, bad news today. God has finally had enough of you. He has had enough of this wicked old world, and He wants you all to know that He is not pleased with you at all, because for the past four hundred years already now in Israel, He has shut up. He hasn't even said anything because He is so angry He is speechless! And in that time, as your sins all came up to His nostrils, He has calculated your trespasses, you see, and now He has had enough. He is ready to press the red button now, you see. It is doomsday, it is now judgment day, judgment day is upon you all, and it is now all over for this world!'*

But NO! The angels came to announce,

"Glad tidings of great joy, which shall be to all the people!"

They came to declare, *"Glory to God in the highest degree possible,"* because He is saying, *"In spite of what you deserve, I do not declare retribution and damnation. I am speaking peace on earth, peace and good will from Me, God, towards all men, towards all of Mankind, in whom I am well pleased! I am declaring to you that I am well pleased with Mankind!"*

It was not at all the message we were expecting! **But God wasn't speaking from our perspective, *He was speaking from His eternal perspective.***

Even in the Scriptures from way back in ancient times, He was already speaking prophetically from a perfect perspective. *He already saw and prophetically declared **our release** in the self-sacrifice of His Son. That release, **our release,** is the fruit of the travail of His own soul.* He already revealed **the joy that was set before Him <u>because He already</u>**

<u>saw</u> *the impact of redemption.* He already knew the impact that would be made in the resurrection, **and it pleased Him!** *He already saw the human race* **rescued and fully restored to our original design.** *The Father* <u>*already saw*</u> *His kids reconciled and returning to His bosom,* **and it pleased Him! We pleased Him! In His everlasting favor towards you, in His everlasting love for you,** *He has always been pleased with you!* *He knows the truth about you, He knows who you are.* **You are His, you are His offspring, and He is pleased with you,** *no matter how deceived or confused you may be.* *No matter how lost we've been,* **we have always been His and <u>He has always loved us</u>**!

We may have lost our way, *but God has never lost sight of us!* He has never lost sight *of our true design,* **no matter how messed up we may be, and how distorted that design has become.** He knows us better than we know ourselves, *and He has always been pleased with us, and He has never stopped loving us* **as His very own dear children!**

We are the very apple of His eye!

What motivates God's favor towards us?

God is a faith God, amen! By faith God saw the fruit of the Lamb. By faith He saw the effect of the blood of His Son. By faith *He saw our redemption completed,* **before it ever**

happened in time. **And He favored us based on that!**

Do you remember how there in Matthew 8:16 Matthew says about Jesus how, *"He cast out the spirits with a word, and healed all who were sick"?*

He goes on to say in verse 17, *"This was to fulfill what was spoken by the prophet Isaiah, 'He took our infirmities and bore our diseases.'"*

Notice how Matthew said, *"This was to fulfill what was spoken by the prophet Isaiah..."*

Now this was long before Jesus went to the cross. This was still during Jesus' ministry before His death. And yet Matthew says, *"This was to fulfill what was spoken by the prophet Isaiah, 'He took our infirmities and bore our diseases.'"*

Can you see that Jesus had a faith-ministry? **Jesus ministered by faith as if He had already died.** Now if Jesus ministered these things by faith, *in such authority* **as if redemption was already a done deal,** how confident can we not be *in ministering in that same authority, that same faith* **based on the now finished work of redemption,** because Isaiah made it absolutely plain that,

"He was despised and rejected **by men**; *a man of sorrows, and acquainted with grief; and as one* **from whom men hide their faces**

he was despised (by men, **not God**), *and **we esteemed him not.***"

"**BUT** *SURELY he has borne our griefs (kholee, sicknesses) and carried our sorrows (makob, pains); yet **we** esteemed him stricken, smitten by God, and afflicted. BUT* (in all reality) *he was wounded for our transgressions* (to rescue our hearts and minds from such foolish thinking and such foolish behavior), *he was bruised for our iniquities* (to rescue us from guilt and shame and the feelings and expectation of condemnation); *upon him was the chastisement that* (we required, not God! What He did in His inexplicable act of love for us) ***made us whole, and thus with his stripes we are healed.***" - Isaiah 53:3-5

The Hebrew word, **kholee** (sickness) is from, **chalab:** *to be weak, sick, or afflicted.*

Isaiah 53:5 ends with: *"...and thus with his stripes **we are healed.**"*

I say again that Jesus, in His ministry on earth as a man, ***ministered in such authority, by faith, as if He had already died!*** **He saw it as a done deal before it even happened!**

Now we as the church, as believers in that work of redemption, as the body of Christ, **can minister in that same authority** Jesus ministered in. We can minister **in that same faith** Jesus ministered in, ***because it already***

happened, *amen,* ***He died****, amen!* **He already died!**

Jesus ministered as if His death and resurrection *weren't some future events!* Jesus ministered as if His death, as if His offering up of Himself, as if His resurrection was already <u>a right now reality</u>! He operated in the prophetic-perfect-tense!

In Mark 11:23 it says that, *"When you pray, believe that you **have** received it, and it shall be yours."* It was written in the aurest-tense, in the prophetic-perfect-tense. That means you have the prophetic insight and confidence; **the faith,** *that what you have prayed for,* **has already been granted, it has already happened!**

Many translators just couldn't get themselves to actually translate it that way, even though that is the correct interpretation from the Greek, because they said that it seemed just too bold! To them it was unthinkable to say it that way, *'I mean, how can anyone say something or pray something with such confidence and finality?!'*

We can! *B***ecause we know our Father's love for us, and because our sin is taken out of the way,** **it is taken care of, it is obliterated by His love for us displayed in that work of redemption.**

It's a done deal, amen!

Redemption is not something off in the future that is yet to come. **It is a reality, amen! It's a done deal! It's already a reality in the heavens, amen! It cannot be reversed; therefore it is a perpetual reality!**

Hallelujah!

So according to the prophetic-perfect tense, according to **the faith of God,** *as far as God is concerned,* the favor which Mary was greeted with, **the favor pronounced upon Mankind** by the angelic hosts, **was already a reality in the heavenlies,** *in the unseen realm of spirit-reality!*

Hallelujah!

Listen God wasn't gambling! God wasn't gambling when He approached Abraham either. No, He saw something, *some reality which already existed,* some ingredient in Abraham's spirit, just like in that young virgin girl, Mary's spirit. **He saw a capacity for faith within their spirits.**

He saw that they were ready to receive the declaration of God and to respond positively to the declaration of God.

He saw this capacity within them *because He knew their design, and He knew their hearts.* **He knew they would yield to the echo of their hearts.** He also knew the power of His word. When God decrees, *He also creates!*

Humanity is absolutely faith compatible! God made us faith compatible!

And so then, when the gospel comes, when the deceleration of God comes, *it creates its own capacity for faith.* You see, the gospel does not demand faith, **it supplies and quickens it!**

Remember Galatians 2:3?

"How did you receive the Spirit? Was it by the works of the law, or did you receive the Spirit by hearing with faith?"

How do we enter into this: *"...hearing with faith?"*

I mean, **how is my faith response quickened** *so that I can now enter into that realm of the supernatural?*

...And this may all sound a bit heady to you right now, but listen to me please. It is not that difficult, it is quite simple, really. I guarantee you that, *as you begin to lay a hold of these truths and begin to thoroughly comprehend and understand them* **and live them in your life as reality; you will begin to witness the supernatural in your life on a daily basis.**

You will just find yourself beginning to live your life *in that realm* **where there is a constant witness of God in your spirit,** *a constant witness of His reality, of His presence and of* *who He is,* **and of His very nearness and person,** *which will begin to spread like a fragrance through you.*

And that fragrance, that witness, will begin to make life and ministry so much easier for you, because, you know, we've labored so long and hard under religion, under man-made religion, and we have fasted and travailed so many wasted days, **but God wants us to enter into the very realm of reality itself,** *into the very faith of God!* He wants us to enter into that reality of faith, into the reality of the law of identification, into the reality *of the work of redemption.* **He wants us to take the liberty of agreeing with God.** *He wants you to take your liberty to agree with Him!*

It is the greatest liberty you can ever take a hold of and partake of: *To come into agreement with the Most High, to line yourself up with what God said, and is still saying, in Jesus Christ, in the gospel.*

God wants us to line ourselves up with what He says in the gospel, **to say with Him** *that it is indeed a reality, that it is indeed great joy to all the earth.*

He desires us to agree that this redemption was accomplished for everyone, that *it is for everyone!*

Chapter 6

The Gospel Came to Replace the Law

"O favored one..."

I can't get that phrase out of my spirit! I can't get enough of God's greeting, of God's deceleration there in Luke 1:28!

"And he came to her (Mary) *and said to her, 'Hail o favored one!"*

You see, some of you need to put yourselves in Mary's place right now. Too many of us read this passage and think, *'Well, it's wonderful for Mary,'* while you continue to condemn yourself and continue to put yourself outside of God's favor! Listen; while you live that way, while you continue to put yourself outside of God's favor, *you are insulting the gospel of Jesus Christ and the Spirit of Grace!*

While you continue to condemn yourself, *you are insulting God!*

If you put yourself outside of God's favor, you are actually saying to Him, *'God, I do not believe the gospel! I do not believe*

redemption is a reality! I do not believe that what Jesus accomplished is a reality!

You are actually saying to God that *Jesus did not pay a high enough price. He didn't pay a price with enough merit in it!*'

You are saying, 'God, Your gift of Your Son, and what He did for me, to take away my sins, was an utter failure!'

How is that for bold confrontation in the spirit of the New Testament! Ha... Ha... Ha...

If you continue to entertain a guilt consciousness, if you continue to entertain a sin-consciousness, and condemnation, and you think, *'Well, this thing of God's favor is not for me, it's not quite for me. God's favor might be for Mary, but not for me.'* I want you to know, yes, you, who are reading this book, even you might be thinking that way, and I want you to know that God is speaking to you right now. God is speaking to you in this book, and He wants you to know His favor. God is speaking to you, right now, and He is greeting you, saying, *"**Hail, o favored one!**"*

God knows where He is coming from when He greets you that way. You see, in the mind of God, in the mind of Justice, in the mind of Him who is love, **your sins are already blotted out!** He is saying, *'**Favor upon you!**'*

*"**Hail, o favored one!**"*

When I read that passage there in Luke 1:28, **I had no option but to come to that conclusion.** You see, I was forced to come to that conclusion, because when I asked the question, *'God, what was it in Mary that caused You to favor her? Was it the works of the law?'* (Because you see, as far as we knew in our old school theology, until that time of Mary, the law was still the only approach that man had to God. Man could only approach God upon the merit of the law, or so we thought and believed.) But what was it that drew the attention of the Most High upon this young virgin girl? Was it her merit that she had earned? Was it the law that counted in her favor? *Or was it the grace of God* **that began to operate in the fullness of time <u>on our behalf</u>?**

It was the grace of God I tell you! Nothing but the grace of God! *The grace of God towards us came into operation there,* **because God had already, before time even began, begun to recognize our association with His Son.** He had already begun to recognize the credit of His Son, the merit of His death and resurrection *in releasing us,* **and so He favored Mary, *He favored her with our favor!*** And you see, if this is not the platform of the gospel, then not one of us has any opportunity to come any closer, or gain any ground, or to go even one inch further, than where we were at in the past, under the Law.

If the gospel still had to somehow lean upon the law, *then the gospel would be made void!*

The gospel did not come to just patch up the law where the law failed! It did not come as an add on to the law. *It came as its replacement!* **The gospel came to** *fulfill* **the law,** *and bring it to its end.* **I say again: The gospel is the law's fulfillment,** *and thus the gospel brings the law to its end.*

Let me say it one more time: **The gospel came to replace religion and bring it to an end!**

Romans 10:4 confirms what I am saying,

*"****Christ is the end of the law,*** **(He is the end of religion)** *for everyone who believes the gospel!"*

He talks about being justified, that *it's exclusively a faith thing now.* **A new dispensation begins in Christ. A new dispensation is introduced through the gospel, through the hearing of faith, and through our hearing with faith! We are living in a new dispensation! A dispensation called: In Christ Jesus!**

You see, because in Christ Jesus the grace of God begins to operate in Man's favor. In Christ Jesus the grace of God begins to introduce fallen Man back into a standing of

righteousness with their God, their Daddy, who loves them. We now live under the smile and the approval of the Most High, of the Most Holy One, the One who loves us with all He is and all He has!

You are His favored ones! The favor of God has got nothing to do with your performance! The favor of God has got nothing to do with the law! It has nothing to do with religion! The favor of God has everything to do with God, with who He is, with His love for us, with the merit of the cross and the resurrection! It stands upon the merits of God's own character! The favor of God stands, it is rooted within the merits, of the gift of Himself within His Son Jesus Christ! He came in person! He came on your behalf, and for you, to win you back and to love you, to favor you, amen! God counts today upon the merits of the performance of Jesus Christ, and not upon your merits under the law, under religion, amen! Are you beginning to appreciate that you, too, are a favored one?

You see, this knowledge is the only knowledge that can get you to enter into that life that is more than just the ordinary. **So I am warning you now that if you stumble over this step, over this knowledge, *then you will never get another step closer.*** You will continue to read books, and study, and sit there in your church, and be a bench warmer only. You will just sit there, and get more and more frustrated within your perspective religion, and the enemy will continue to load down your mind, with all kinds of stupid ideas, that are generated by and agree with the law. The devil will continue to bog down your heart, with all kinds of criticisms of yourself, which will continue to justify your life of total powerlessness.

But God has made available to us, in the gospel of Jesus Christ, *a power resource **in the person of the Holy Spirit.*** *It's available to us in the person of the Spirit of Truth,* ***who lives and abides within us.***

I say again: God has made available for His Church, for us, every single believer, *a powerhouse of Divine energy, that will mobilize His body, where He dwells in all His fullness,* and turn us into a mighty army, that goes around and reconciles God's kids to Him, while destroying all the works of the enemy. God has made that kind of a life available for every one of us. And I am telling you, there remains no excuse for any one of us to remain ignorant concerning these things.

There really is no excuse for any of us to just wrap ourselves with a nice comfortable blanket of ignorance, and say *'Well, we're quite happy with the life we have lived thus far. We're very content with our slack living, spiritually speaking, we're content with the religion of our own making, and with just the little evidence of the supernatural we've seen in our lives so far. We're content with such little evidence of the reality and power of God in our lives.'*

I am telling you now in this book that in this time we live in today, *we are living in a time where the gospel is being clarified and made plain, perhaps like never before.* We are living in such a time where God is challenging His Church, challenging us as individual believers, and bringing us to a threshold. He is challenging us again and again *to step over that threshold* **into that spirit dimension,** *into that world of* **spirit reality,** *into a new* **experience** *of the supernatural,* **by making fully known to us** *and repeatedly stressing* **the reality of righteousness.**

He's stressing how it totally releases you from a sin-consciousness and from entertaining your past and that old fleshly identity.

And He's emphasizing how it brings you to a place where you step into a new realm of authority with God.

God wants you to lift your head and look into His eyes!

Remember when Peter saw Him and wept when he saw those eyes? He had just denied Him, *but he saw something more.* He saw the **favor**, the **love**, in those eyes! **He saw the favor of God in the eyes of Jesus!**

He knew and remembered and believed what Jesus already declared concerning his future.

Jesus declared,

*'You are a piece of the Rock. Upon this revelation that you've come into now Peter, upon this rock solid foundation **of your true spirit identity,** I will build my Church.'*

*'I will build up and strengthen, with this knowledge, my body, those who become believers, and who embrace this knowledge, whom I will then also be able to indwell by my Spirit. I will strengthen them, and by My Spirit I will build them up with this understanding, the understanding of their righteousness, of their true authentic identity in Me, **and they will go forth and conquer!'***

You see, we really do need to learn to deal with failure. Far too many of us still entertain our failure, and we nurse that thing until it becomes a monster that consumes us. **God wants you to see your failure in the light of His favor *that He has favored you with in Christ!***

Please allow the Spirit of God to deal with you today, right now. Take that failure, take that ugly sin, and say, *'God, I want to sit here and I want to meditate and ponder, by the help of Your Holy Spirit right now. I want to sit here and measure, the merit of my failure, with the merit of Your favor. I want to compare, and I want to see and discover for myself how Your favor overshadows, overwhelms, and throws out my past,* **and cancels it,** *while introducing me to,* **and bring me into,** *newness of living.'*

O favored one, God wants to greet you and embrace you! He wants you to look Him in the eye again! To fellowship face-to-face again, *in the bliss of your absolute innocence* **which He has given to you as a gift!**

He wants you to stop avoiding Him! He wants you to stop pretending, *and living a lie!*

Living a lie is no substitute for the real thing. Living a lie is no substitute to living in the favor of God, *living in the bliss of His favor.* It's no substitute for living in the bliss of intimate fellowship with the living God, the One who favors you, the One who has made you accepted in the Beloved, the One who **truly loves you!**

Chapter 7

Fully Embrace The Gospel!

Jesus said in Acts 1:8 that, *"You shall receive power when the Holy Spirit comes upon you ...when He finds you and you find Him, when you find and discover each other, there in your inner-man; when you encounter the Holy Spirit ...when the Spirit of wisdom and revelation in the knowledge of Him comes to you, when the Spirit of truth comes and He begins to **saturate your inner-man,** and His nearness becomes **a reality,** and He begins to rise up within you **and overwhelms you from within,** with who He is, and who I am, in you, and so you shall **be** My witnesses, in Jerusalem, and all of Judea, and in all of Samaria, and to the uttermost remote parts of the earth; even to the very ends of the earth!"*

He was prophesying!

You see; when the Spirit of Truth begins to quicken the truth within you, *He begins to awaken and unlock* **those fountains of the deep, those rivers of living water** *inside of you, inside your spirit,* and something begins to happen in your heart and in your spirit, *and you are revolutionized on the inside, and from the inside out!*

Listen, if you want to come into the realm of the supernatural, you are going to have to stop considering with your natural mind, *'I wonder if it's going to be too embarrassing for me to do this and to do that? I wonder if everybody is going to start staring at me if I start to do this or if I do that? I wonder if somebody is going to look at me funny if I do this or that?'*

You are going to have to forget about the world, and forget about yourself, and you are going to have to yield to that which is stirring within you, that which is rising up within your spirit. *It's the working of the Holy Spirit,* **it's the love of God quickened; stirred up within you!**

You are going to have to yield and become bold if you want to come into that realm, *into that life of the supernatural.*

If you want to begin to walk in the reality of the supernatural, in the reality of living life with the Spirit of God, you are going to have to crucify those ideas in your mind, those feelings that make you feel a little bit uncomfortable when things start to get a little emotional, or start to get a little loud and passionate! Crucify those feelings, those thoughts that make you feel embarrassed and make you blush with shame and draw back, when it's time to enter in, or when it's time to get bold! Listen, you are going to have to die to those things, *those soul-realm things.* Otherwise they will take you to your grave; *they will kill you spiritually speaking!* They will imprison you to the flesh *and to a life that is void of the Divine witness!*

...Because you see, Jesus says in Acts 1:8 that, **"You will receive power,** *when the Holy* **Spirit comes,** *when you encounter Him,* <u>*when the Spirit of Truth rises up from within you*</u> *and stirs you up in the love of God!"*

He says, **"You <u>shall</u> receive power** ...and *you* <u>shall be</u> *My witnesses!"*

Listen, that power is not intimidated by the principalities, by the power of darkness. It's not intimidated by any governing power, nor by any government of this world! That power is not intimidated by human criticism or any human response that is negative! That spirit within you is not motivated by human applause, it is not motivated by the praise of Man, nor the lack thereof. It doesn't live for the praise of Man! All it cares about is the praise of God, to live to the praise of His glory. It's not trying to still obtain that praise, but it lives *from that praise,* **knowing that you already have the praise and the approval of God! You already have the favor of God!**

That power is a boldness within your spirit *which God births in your heart,* **as you begin to grasp and believe the love of God for all people.** It's birthed in you, as you truly believe,

107

as you truly grasp, the knowledge of God, the knowledge of your redemption, and Mankind's redemption, *and believe it on a deeper level,* not just in your intellect, not just in your mind, *but deep down in your heart, in your spirit!*

That power is a boldness in your spirit *which God births in your heart,* **as you begin to believe the word, as you truly believe the gospel!**

Believe the word!

Believe the gospel!

Believe that word, believe that message, believe that gospel that is revealed in the Scriptures, and say, *'God, let it be unto me according to your word!'*

You see, there was Mary in Luke 1:29, considering what this sort of greeting might mean, *'Hail o favored one!'* She was considering it in her heart. And after fully considering it in her heart, she responded and said, *"Let it be unto me according to Your word!"* - Luke 1:38

There are many today considering, *'What is this gospel? You know, this gospel of grace we are hearing these days, is it a new gospel? Is it, you know, an easy free ride for all? It is not, perhaps, you know, just another gospel that excuses sin and makes light of sin, another fake righteousness that falls short, you know, a righteousness that will also fail us and not produce the kind of power necessary for real change and real transformation; a real walk of intimacy and purity with God?'*

Listen man, for those of you that are always harping on repentance and our need for repentance, emphasizing that we need to teach repentance the way Jeremiah did, and you always emphasize that John the Baptist and that Jesus also preached repentance. Listen, you fail to grasp that real repentance, the word: **Metanoia**, in the Greek, has to do with our wrong religious opinions that need to be changed!

The Latin word, *repentance,* refers to *penance,* and penance implies a payment of some sort. Many cathedrals of old, as well as present day religious organizations, are financed by this concept of guilt and paying for your sins. Thus a person's own depth of sincerity, or feelings of regret, and *'acts of penance',* as prescribed by those who tout repentance, *become their own atonement for sins.* This mistranslation of the word, **metanous** or **metanoia** has led to great error and misunderstanding. The Latin word, re-penance, literally means *a repetition of penance.*

Now the original Greek word used in the Scriptures, **Metanoia**, literally means **to intelligently, thoroughly understand; to come to your senses; to come into your**

109

right mind. It has to do with coming face to face with truth, and thus changing your opinion about the matter at hand. It has to do with discarding any wrong opinions you have held to, prior to a more accurate understanding of a subject. It has to do with coming to an accurate conclusion about something, and coming into agreement with that truth discovered. Thus, **Metanoia** has to do with changing your mind and coming into agreement with God on something, because the opinion you previously held to was inaccurate. You were mistaken; you were of the wrong opinion, until God opened your eyes to it and revealed to you the truth.

I say again: **Metanoia** has to do with the fact that I have to change my opinion and agree with God!

Tell me, when the gospel comes to you, when the actual gospel comes to you *accurately,* the **true gospel,** *as God sees it and knows it,* what kind of opinion is introduced to you?

An opinion that causes you to shrink back?

I think not!

I do not believe that shrinking back is the fruit of the gospel! It may be the fruit of man's gospel, *but it is not the fruit of God's gospel.*

The fruit, the impact of God's true gospel is reconciliation, a drawing nigh, not a drawing back or a shrinking back in shame!

True repentance, true **Metanoia,** has to do with my opinion that I have to change: **The opinion that I am filthy!** I have to change that opinion about myself, in light of the gospel, in light of Christ's accomplishment on my behalf, and for me.

True **Metanoia** is an adjustment in your thinking, in favor of and towards an opinion that concentrates on the gospel, and on the favor of God. Because you see, the gospel is the favor message. It is the message of favor; it is the message of God's favor! **The gospel is the message of the favor, of that very favor, that is in the heart of God towards this world,** *towards everyone, including you!*

Paul had the revelation in Romans 1:16, that this gospel is no meek little thing. What God accomplished in Christ Jesus wasn't just a poor effort of God, to try and con the world into getting into His kingdom. No, this gospel, says Paul, is the very power of God unto true righteousness. **It's the power of God!** It's not just clever speech, and it's not just another weak little compromised message, by which we tell people, *'Don't worry. If you're just a bunch of sinners, don't worry, it will be alright. You know God will accept you for who you are in your opinion of yourself in the flesh.'*

No that is not what we preach!

That is not what the gospel proclaims!

The gospel is the power of God that *concentrates on His favor.*

And you know what that kind of focus and revelation does? You know what that kind of repentance, that **Metanoia** does? *It changes your opinion of God **and of yourself!***

It changes your opinion!

Where before you thought of yourself in terms of the Law, you thought of yourself in terms of your past failures. Your opinion about yourself was, *'Ugh, man, as far as religion is concerned, as far as God is concerned, I'm a miserable pitiable person. I'm no good, and I have no approach before God, so I'll just continue in my own self-righteous pride, and in my rebellion against Him!'*

But suddenly now your mind is changed because of the gospel, a new revelation dawns upon your spirit and impacts your heart, because you realize that the gospel says, *'You are favored; you're favored man, you're FAVORED!'*

Hallelujah!

And that favor, the favor of God, begins to dawn upon you, *and an explosion of joy happens within your spirit.* Joy comes to you, unspeakable joy, and full of glory. It's the kind of joy that overwhelms you emotionally because you realize that, *'Man, He has wiped out the handwriting of requirements that stood against me! He has nailed it to the cross* **so it can die!** *He has* **canceled** *my sins,* **He has removed them from me as far away as far away can be;** <u>**as far as the east is from the west**</u>**!** **He has removed them! He blotted out my transgressions! He doesn't hold my trespasses against me!***'*

That favor draws me to God. That favor brings sonship: the very witness of the Spirit that bears witness with my spirit that *I am indeed a child of God!*

My past teachers may not bear witness with what I understand right now. My professors of theology might not agree; *religion might not agree.* But listen, if the Spirit of God **comes into agreement with the truth I've heard, with the truth of the gospel, and there is a witness brought into your spirit** that says, *you're alright, you are qualified* ...that Holy spirit witness to the truth of the gospel says in your spirit that, if anyone accepts the truth, and embraces these things, *that God gives them the legal right to feel like, and behave like, to become* **the children of God,** <u>**those very children He proclaims and reveals them to be**</u>**!**

...if that Spirit of God witnesses within your spirit and says these things, **then who cares about the opinion of religion?** Who cares what my teachers and professors think?!

And then you know, *once you have embraced that witness,* **over the witness of man, over any other opinion,** then what happens next?

Then that witness begins to rule over all the evidence of your past, that whole dirty old record of who you were, and what you did, and what you were involved in! *It is canceled, it is blotted out, it is obliterated!*

"*If* **therefore** *any man is in Christ,* (if he finds and discovers himself in Christ, he finds that) *he is a new creation, the old things have passed away,* **behold the new has come!**"
- 2 Corinthians 5:17

Listen, in the light of that reality, in the light of discovering yourself in Christ, in the light that God has revealed you to be in Christ, in the light of *beholding the new that has come*, in that light, *everything becomes new, it becomes new,* **brand new!**

God wants us all to enjoy that newness of life! It is what Jesus died for! *It's what He died for!*

Chapter 8

Agree with God!

We have been so conditioned by the Law and by man-made religion. But today I am telling you, here in this book, God says, *"Now as you have received Christ, walk in Him!"* Paul says, *"Let us now walk in Him; as you have received Christ, so walk in Him!"* - Colossians 2:6

How did you receive Him? Did you receive Jesus through the works of the Law, after you had obeyed all the commandments and jumped through all the hoops, you know, when you had God really impressed with how diligent you were in praying and fasting and doing all those little things? Did you receive Him after you finally had God's attention and God's well done and God's applause, and so God said to you, *'Well done, you know, thou good and Law-keeping servant!'?*

No? Then how did you receive Christ?

Was it through the works of the law, *or by **the hearing of faith?***

You receive Christ through the hearing of faith, amen! You received by hearing and believing the love God has for you, and by relying on that love. As you have received Christ, so walk in Him! Do not begin in the spirit and end up in the flesh again! Do not begin in the faith of God and end up under the law again! As you have received Christ, so walk in Him! So walk in Him! It's a faith thing, it's a hearing of faith thing from start to finish! We are dealing with the faith of God! It's not by the works of the law; *its by hearing with faith!*

That same principle applies to walking in the Spirit. Walking in the supernatural is the same principle. It works by the same principle, the principle of faith. It's so simple, but it's so dynamic, it's so profound, because it's the faith of God we operate in; *it's the heart of God revealed, it's the gospel of His Son, amen!*

*"**Hail o favored one!**"* - Luke 1:28

What sort of profound greeting must this be?

I want you to continue to weigh this greeting! Weigh this greeting from the heart of God. **Weigh it in your own heart.** *Don't weigh it with what you've been used to hearing under religion, and with what you've been taught in the past.* Don't weigh it with some of your favorite condemnation preachers and fear-mongers who scream out your sins! *Don't weigh it with your favorite preacher's messages and opinions expressed.* **Don't even weigh it with that!** It cannot be weigh and compared with Old Testament doctrine and man-made teachings; *with religion.* This greeting, this declaration from God is to profound for that! **Rather weigh it, and compare it, *with the heart of God expressed in Christ.* Compare it with the heart of God expressed in the gospel of your salvation; expressed there *in the one and only true gospel!***

"Hail o favored one!" - Luke 1:28

This greeting, this profound declaration over us, over you, **comes from above, it comes straight from the mouth of God, it comes from the mind of God and the heart of God, it comes *directly from the fountainhead!***

So, stop drinking downstream! That water, that message, those hand-me-downs, those doctrines, those customs and traditions and beliefs and opinion of our ignorant forefathers, that old time religion, that poor excuse of a gospel that was handed down to us through ages and generation, *is contaminated and polluted! It is toxic and poisonous; mere opinions of men, it is no gospel at all!*

When God greeted us with, *"***Hail o favored one!***"* when He made that profound declaration over us, **He introduced the true gospel!**

Hey listen; God foresaw in His Son the just requirement of the Law *fulfilled!* He saw that handwriting that stood against us, with all its legal demands, and with all its accusations, *nailed to that cross.* **He saw it done away with! *He himself brought it to an end!* Christ is the end of the Law!**

Your condemnation of yourself will not add anything to your salvation! It will not be able to add anything! It will not add to the merit of the cross, to the merit of Jesus, to that merit of His work of redemption! There is no redeeming merit in your condemnation of yourself! **Your condemnation of yourself is not a sign of humility; it's a sign of stupidity!** *It's a sign of ignorance!*

But listen, when I hear the true gospel of Jesus, I stop insulting Him and I begin to agree with God. I say, *'God I agree with You! I agree with what You say! And You say* **I'm your favored one!** *So I say I***'m Your favored one! God I'm Your favored one!'**

Hallelujah!

...And all the while I'm considering, *"What sort of greeting is this?"*

Let me tell you, *I'm going to consider this greeting. I'm going to consider it, I'm going to consider this revelation. I'm considering that I am indeed His favored one.*

That's right, *I'm going to consider what sort of gospel this is. I am going to consider, what exactly the gospel is. I'm considering where exactly it comes from, where it originated.*

...And where is it coming from?

It is coming directly from God! It comes from God Himself!

So, I'm considering and discovering that *it originates in the heart of God.* **It comes from the very heart of God.** It's God's gospel, **it comes from Him!**

It is different from Jeremiah's message, it's different from Moses' message, it's different from the Old Covenant, **completely different!**

Hey listen; **This message, this gospel is God's revelation of Himself and of us, of His righteousness and of our righteousness.**

So you bet your bottom dollar I am going to consider where this gospel comes from!

I am going to consider what sort of greeting this is: "...**and on the earth, <u>peace</u>**..." - Luke 2:14

'Come on God, please, You must be joking, You haven't heard the latest news reports yet!'

"...**on the earth, <u>peace</u> ...for in humanity I am well pleased**..."

'Wow Rudi, but that's not what my pastor says about the human race and about this earth. That's not my pastor's take on things...'

'...He said just this past Sunday, "Just wait and see folks, God's still going to punish America, He's going to pour His wrath out upon this nation, and upon the whole world; upon us all!"'

'...And now you see, we are cringing and we are ducking again at the mere remembrance of his sermon, and so now our whole attitude towards God is one of just staying out of His way. We are full of the fear of God, and so now we will just stay out of His way, and fear what is coming to this earth. We fear what is coming our way!'

Listen, America has been lied to! The world has been lied to! The whole world needs to hear the true gospel, *America included!*

That gospel, that true gospel, the gospel of God, as announced by the angels, and by Jesus, by Paul and by all the rest of the New Testament apostles also, and not the so called *"gospel"* we have heard, but the gospel they announced, **is the power of God unto salvation and unto wholeness!** That gospel, the true gospel of God, *will introduce you to and usher you into,* **the life of the supernatural!**

It is high time that America and the world consider what kind of greeting this is in Luke Chapter Two!

Hey listen, we who preach the grace of God in truth, we are not a strange group of people *with a new message.* This message we proclaim is the original gospel, the golden oldie, the gospel of Jesus Christ that has been around *from the beginning!*

I've heard some preachers say, "*It's time that we get back to the good old days, to the time when we used to sing, 'Just give me that old time religion!' It's time that we get back to preaching hell-fire and brimstone! It's time for the church to start preaching repentance again!*"

No listen; forget about them good old days. That's too old. That's Moses, that's the Old Testament! **The New has come! A greater than Moses has come!** We don't need to go back to the good old days, to our roots, to that old time religion, to our traditions and customs handed down by our ignorant forefathers. NO, we need to go further back, back to Jesus and Paul and the incarnation and the New Testament!

It's time for us to get back to the true gospel!

Stop preaching your church's favorite doctrine and traditions! Stop preaching Moses! It's not the day of Moses. **It's the day of Jesus!** It's not the day of religion; **it's the day of Jesus!**

It's not the day of Moses; it's the day of the Joshua generation *that will take God's people **into newness of living!***

It is Joshua that caused God's people to inherit the land, not Moses! Under Moses they just sat there and scratched their sores in the wilderness, and felt condemned, and so they mumbled and grumbled in the wilderness, *'This is all we have, you know, God did speak about a land, but maybe it's only after death that we are going to get into this land, but in the meantime, brother, it's all just a wilderness experience. It's all just dust, we're trying to cope and eke out a living in this dust. That's all we have, that's all we are left with in this life, trying to deal with dust!'* And so, just like the Israelites of old, we have identified ourselves with dust, *and we have been insulting the gospel in our preaching of it!*

Listen; let us not also die *in the wilderness!*

Let us not die in a wilderness of our own making, **when the truth of the gospel has been so clearly revealed and proclaimed!**

Let us not be ignorant any longer, but let us continue to consider what sort of greeting this is here in Luke 1:30,

"*And then the angel said to her* (to Mary)*, **do not be afraid***..."

Where does fear come from? Why did He have to tell her not to fear?

Because fear has to do with punishment. She was a woman under the Law, afraid of punishment! She was living in sin-consciousness along with everyone else in her life and in her generation!

As long as we live that way, every crisis that comes our way is, *'O, that's God judging me again. You know, I may have slipped up somewhere, so let me just go and check up quickly in the Law and scrutinize myself. Yup, I certainly must be falling short somewhere.' So here we go, 'God, You just go ahead and do what You must, what You've got to do, I'll just reap what I've sown.'*

But inside I resent Him, and I say, *'But you know, God, my brother has done worse things than I've done, and yet here You are getting me for it, and the same things aren't befalling him.'*

And the devil laughs all the way. Because you know what he does? He destroys the plan of God for your life, *driving in a wedge between you and God,* so that every time you come into God's presence *you feel uncomfortable.*

Every time the Holy Spirit begins to move *you feel uncomfortable* and you want to avoid it, you just as soon stay outside of such an encounter and stay away *because it scares you.*

Listen, use this book to help you deal with that religious root of fear in your heart and life!

Let the Spirit of God show you *the true heart of God.* Let Him show you *His favor* **towards you!** Let Him show you His favor today!

Religion always preaches, *'Let God show you yourself, you know, because the Holy Spirit will convict you of sin.'*

And religion had us convinced in our minds that the Holy Spirit when He comes will show your whole past to you. He will show you what a little dirty old sinner you've been, so that you can repent, and build up enough grief over these things, over who you are, so that you could eventually, hopefully, change enough, to maybe escape hell and make it into heaven one day, *maybe.* That's been the religious, so called, *"gospel"* approach.

Listen, **that's not the ministry of the Holy Spirit.**   That's the ministry of religion, the ministry of the Law! Paul calls it the ministry of death! - 2 Corinthians 3:7.

There in the book of John, (John 16:8-11) John talks about the ministry of the Holy Spirit and he says that the Holy Spirit will *"convict us of sin, righteousness, and Judgment."* But then, just in case we misunderstand what he is trying to say with a legalistic, bound-up-in-the-law, religiously-trained mind, he clarifies what he is saying about the Spirit of Truth right afterwards. It is as if Jesus interjects His own little commentary there, and this is what He say, He says, *"Of sin, because you did not believe in Me!"* - John 16:9

...Not because God calculated and added up all kinds of things that you did, both the big and little things that you did, and is holding it against you, but because you rejected Jesus, who is love personified, and you rejected the truth about yourself as it is revealed in Jesus!

Listen; if you have a problem with LOVE, then you really have a problem!

The only sin that can cause you to still remain outside is the sin of rejecting Jesus, the sin of rejecting LOVE, the sin of rejecting the truth as it is revealed in Jesus and that work of redemption! **Your own rejection keeps you outside, *not God!* God doesn't keep you outside, *you do!***

Why can I say that with such confidence?

Because He already took your sin, He already took all our transgressions under the Law upon Himself, *and He nailed it to the cross.* **He took it out of the way and He obliterated it there!**

I say again: **Your own rejection *keeps you outside*, not God! God doesn't keep you outside, *you do!***

*"...And of righteousness, because I go to the Father ...**so that we could be where He is!***" - John 16:10/John 14:3

"...And of judgment..." - John 16:11 Because God is now going to get me? Because God is still out to get me? NO!

*"...And of judgment, **because the ruler of this world has been judged!**"* - John 16:11

Amen! Hallelujah!

God didn't step out of eternity into time to judge you. He didn't come to judge you; *He came to judge the devil!* **He already judged and rendered powerless the ruler of this world!**

There is no need to fear the devil! There is no need to give him any more authority than God says he has. God says he has none! The enemy has been defeated and disarmed in the work of redemption! Why preach a defeated foe back into business again?! *"If God is for us, who can be against us!"* - Romans 8:31-39.

There is no need to fear the devil anymore! And hey, there is no need to fear the God who is love, who demonstrated His love for us, either!

The conviction of the Spirit wants to bring into your heart *an understanding, **an appreciating** of the gospel of **the favor of God.** In that favor God says to us,* "**Do not be afraid!**" - Luke 1:30

You see, my approach to God used to be always motivated by fear. So I had to do a creepy crawly on God, ha... ha... ha... you know, *'I bow and I crawl before you Lord, forgive me, I'm a miserable sinner, I plead for mercy...'*

And religion trains its people to do this Sunday after Sunday, week in and week out. But Paul says, in 2 Corinthians 3:15 that, *"Even to this day, whenever Moses is read, that same veil* (that same ignorance, that same cloud of condemnation and confusion) *remains unlifted."*

Sunday after Sunday they read the Law, and they stand by that law, and everybody, like a parrot, repeats after the minister and sings a little phrase, *'You know, we have transgressed Your Law – We have O God, Your Law transgressed. Mercy is all we plead for.'*

And in the meantime they are all bored out of their minds and sitting there thinking of yesterday's golf game! And they keep pleading for God's mercy Sunday after Sunday, *because they are so ignorant of the gospel!* And they are still living under Moses, and living under the Law, *and busy with their own religion.* And multitudes upon multitudes in every nation are in captivity *to ignorance.* They live their lives *in captivity to ignorance!*

But God says to us, and to you who read this book, *'Lift up your voice with strength!'* He says, *'Don't whisper the Gospel! Now that you know the gospel, don't whisper the gospel!* ***Get into that boldness, already residing within your Spirit!'***

God says, ***'Get into that boldness!'*** He says, *'You shall receive power when the Holy Spirit comes and He stirs within you!* ***He will empower you with a boldness*** *to be a witness of Jesus,* ***to be a witness for this gospel!*** *He will empower you to boldly challenge the people, to challenge them* ***with the true gospel of the favor of God,*** *to challenge* ***the deception*** *this world has had to bow its knee to for way too long. Religious lies and deception has kept this world in bondage up to now!'* But God says, *"**<u>Do not be afraid, for you have found favor with God</u>**!"* - Luke 1:30

Can you see that once Luke started meditating upon this, and pondering upon it, and considering it, he couldn't get away from it either! Ha... ha.... ha...

Luke 1:31-34,

"And behold you shall conceive in your womb, and bear a son, and you shall call his name Jesus."

"He will be great, and will be called the Son of the Most High; and the Lord God will give to him the throne of his father David, and he will reign over the house of Jacob forever; and of his kingdom there will be no end!"

"And Mary said to the angel, 'How shall this be...'"

This is the very question we are exploring today and answering in this book.

"How shall these things be?"

"And Mary said to the angel, 'How shall this be, since I have no husband?'"

You see the plans she had for her future did not at this stage include this miracle. She was prepared to just be *another ordinary woman,* to bear children to her husband, Joseph, to settle down somewhere, away from the big city of Jerusalem, fraught with danger, and full of treacherous politics, and live perhaps in a quaint and quiet little town like Bethlehem in Nazareth, *where life would be nice and comfortable.* She wanted to be, *just an ordinary housewife.*

But listen, I want you to know today that the Holy Spirit has in mind for ordinary housewives *much more* that what you have planned for!

You see, when you begin to experience the favor of God, then suddenly Isaiah 54 begins to speak to you, *"Sing o barren one, enlarge the place of your tent ...enlarge the place of your tent! You are about to conceive! Something supernatural is about to come upon you! Something supernatural is about to happen to you! Something supernatural is about to be deposited within you, and conceived in your spirit, and given birth to in the flesh; in your very life!"*

*"**How shall this be**...?"* - Luke 1:34

*"And the angel said to her, '**The Holy Spirit will come upon you, and the power of the Most High will overshadow you...**'"* - *verse 35.*

*"'...therefore the child to be conceived within you, and born, will be called: **the holy Son of God.**'"*

"'And behold, your kinswoman, Elizabeth, in her old age has also conceived a son (also by faith; by fully embracing God's deceleration over her)*; and this is the sixth month with her who was called barren.'"*

*"'**For no word of God is without power**.'"* - Luke 1:36 & 37.

Some translations say, *"For nothing is impossible with God,"* and that's also true!

But the Greek says, *"No word of God..."* I love the detail of the Greek language, it says, *"**No word of God is void of power!**"*

'...Mary, stop planning for your life in the light of who you are in your natural person! Mary, stop seeing a future for yourself, like any other young girl would see for herself! Stop seeing

the same kind of future for yourself that they see for themselves! **Because the word of God has come to you ...GOD'S WORD HAS COME TO <u>YOU</u>!**'

'Listen; there is a new dimension of living available to you, Mary ...within the word! You can be more than just the ordinary ...you can be more than just one of the community, to just be part of the community …but you can be one that is born from above ...you can be one who walks in that reality ...you can be one who walks in the reality of the supernatural!'

"And Mary said," Verse 38, *'**Let it be to me according to your word.**'"*

She says, *'God, I am Your handmaid, right here and now I turn my back on my identity in the flesh, on all my own plans, on all my own ambitions, on all my own desires for my future.* ***I'm submitting my future to the future that Your word births within me! Let it be to me according to Your word! Let Your word dictate as far as my future is concerned! Let Your word rule my future!***'

And what did the angel say? ***"The Holy Spirit will overshadow you ...He will overshadow you and come upon you ...the very power of the Most High will overshadow you."***

I know I have gotten a little off track in this book, but I know in my heart that God has brought us together to a place where we recognize, and hopefully you do too, that, by the power of the Holy Spirit, God wants to introduce us into a dimension of supernatural living which is far above the ordinary.

I know for sure that God doesn't want His *"church,"* His people who believe in Him, and are trying to associate with Him and identify with Him, to *continue to insult Him by not embracing His gospel.*

He doesn't want us to continue to insult Him *by being content with the ordinary,* with just another ordinary Sunday, going through the religious motions, going through their rituals and customs and traditions, *and expecting yet again another ordinary week.*

He wants us to enlarge our expectations!

Listen, the world might be expecting bloodshed and war, but don't tune in to that my precious brother and sister. Don't tune in to that! If you are indeed a true Christian, don't tune in to politics and the latest political conversation. And turn that television off! You may get offended at me for saying these things, *but if there is ever a time where you need to stop listening to what the television has to say,* ***it is now!***

Listen; get your heart fired up instead, *with the true gospel of Jesus Christ!*

Be like a little infant as far as evil is concerned, man. Don't always try and be the best news reporter out there. **Rather be the best good news reporter, *be the best at reporting God's good news; God's gospel,* amen!**

The Scriptures say in 1 Corinthians 14:20, *"As far as evil is concerned, be guileless. Be like a little infant."*

Little infants, up to one or two years old, *can't be tempted with evil.* You can't tempt that little person with evil; **they are only interested in sincere milk.**

Now here in 1 Corinthians 14:20 God says, *"Be like that. Be just like that little infant!"* It's real simple: **What you feed will grow, *and what you starve will die.***

Some of you reading this book right now might even have to go and check what you are feasting on all the time, *what you are entertained by and feeding off of all the time, and put that thing out of your life!*

If you are reading books and watching material that directly contradict the true gospel you might as well burn it. That's right, **burn it,** *rather than give that filth the time of day and allowing it to hang around your house and your life,* **spreading its influence some more to others who might read it or watch it.** Don't even give it away. Don't even try and sell it or give it to charity, don't even take it to the

Salvation Army or Goodwill for that matter, *just burn it, amen.* **I know this may be way too radical for some of you,** *but lives are at stake!*

Unless we finally get radical and get serious with the gospel, *with impacting our world with the true gospel of God, who else will?*

How else is change for the better ever going to come to this planet, *if we don't start meaning business with the truth of the gospel and getting serious with God!?*

How else can real transformation happen? **It can't amen, it can't!**

It is high time that we start cleansing our hearts and cleaning up our houses again like the early believers did in the book of acts (Acts 19:8-20).

We live in a world today, *created by the zeal of God that was at work within them!* If it wasn't for them, Christianity wouldn't be around today, not even the watered down, compromised, weak, religious version of it we have working, or failing, in our world, depending on your perspective.

Listen, those early believers became radical, *they became empowered by the Holy Spirit* **and radical in their love,** and they took everything related to idolatry, and that which might sponsor demonic activity, *and they burned it.* Because a passion got ignited in their hearts through the gospel, through the love of God, and they wanted to go all out for God **without any more distractions,** *without any other influences still hanging around and working its way back into their minds and hearts, into their thinking.*

They made a heap, and they all danced around that fire as that previously valuable junk burned, *and they bore strong witness to the fact that the works of the devil had been destroyed in their lives.* And so they burned those things through which the devil used to gain entrance and have a hold on their lives, *so that there would be no point of contact left, not even a small window of opportunity for the enemy to gain entrance and a foothold again in their lives.* They destroyed that point of contact and allowed the Spirit of God to find a clean channel straight into their hearts, into their spirits, to magnify the gospel, to magnify the Lord Jesus Christ, to magnify the Most High God. **They allowed Holy Spirit to magnify His love and His truth within them and through them!**

If you allow the Spirit of God access to your heart, to your spirit, through the gospel, *through marinating in the gospel, and magnifying that gospel above all other knowledge, above all other influence and focus in your life,* **you will be brought to the threshold of invading that supernatural realm, that realm of the impossible, where**

the supernatural is natural, where the impossible becomes possible!

If we would only allow the gospel *to live large in our hearts,* and allow the Spirit of God, that Spirit of Truth, *to abide within us,* and to minister to us, and impart to us, and strengthen us, and empower us, *then we would no longer be limited to the realm of possibilities, but we would enter into and taste of the realm of impossibilities.*

I really believe that some of you have been challenged in your heart in the reading of this book. I believe you've been challenged to step out of that comfort zone environment of the flesh you have built for yourself. I believe you have been challenged by the Spirit of God Himself, about being a lazy fisherman *long enough,* and sitting there in your nice little boat *rocking you to sleep.* You have been challenged like Gideon *to stop hiding behind your fears* in the wine-press, in that job you work at, in that job-description you cling to in the natural, just eking out a living for you and yours, merely surviving here on planet earth.

I am not saying quit your job, you zealot you, your workplace is included in your ministry; it's a mission field ripe unto harvest! And no, you are there to work, not to turn your workplace into some church or something! That's the wrong kind of religious mentality! I am not encouraging any of that! All I am saying is that you just need to take that first step in your heart today, that first step of faith, that first step of yielding to God.

It is time for you to get out of the boat, and take a step of faith. It's time for you to get out of your wine-press comfort zone mentality, and it's time to confront your unbelief and your fears and to have an encounter with the Holy Spirit, with the Spirit of Truth!

But listen, that encounter will not just happen, it will not happen to you, it will not follow, *until you hear and comprehend, until you understand fully,* **and hear with faith, what God is truly saying in Christ.**

"How did you receive the Spirit? **Through hearing with faith.**" - Galatians 3:2 & 5.

Hebrews 4:2 says that the good news the Israelites heard in the desert, *"the gospel they heard, did not benefit them,* **because it wasn't mixed together with faith.**"

Don't cheat yourself and think, *'I believe'* just because your mind agrees with the principle.

Listen, that faith is of the Spirit, **it's a total persuasion, it's a conviction that begins to burn in your heart and it burns and burns and burns** *...and it burns away the dross of every lie that has ever come against you and held sway in your life!*

That faith begins to rise up within you. It rises up inside of you and it says, *'The gospel is the truth, it is THE TRUTH!' And I take that word; I take His word for it! I take that promise, that reality, and I receive the promise of the Holy Spirit! And that Holy Spirit of Truth then comes to overshadow and confirm the word of God, the truth of the gospel, with signs and wonders.*

I do believe that in this time we live in, God desires His church to witness, perhaps like never before, the supernatural happen in our lives.

Listen, we need not wait for some big time preacher to come to town and to show off with some supernatural power. Praise God for that, but it's high time for God's desire to be fulfilled, it's high time for every single individual that makes up the body of Christ to witness it. The supernatural is not limited to preaching behind the pulpit. It is for you, right there in your kitchen, right there in your closet.

Mary was in her closet, and there in private the supernatural overshadowed her. **God wants to overshadow you!**

Father I praise You! Jesus we adore You!

I thank you, Holy Spirit, that You've come, commissioned by God, that You've been sent forth from out of heaven, out of that unseen dimension, that realm of spirit reality. Thank you that you've been sent forth from God

Himself, that You proceed from both the Father and the Son, and we are determined in our spirit today, we are determined, we will not be another group of people, another person, that will neglect to recognize Your ministry in our midst, in our own hearts even, here in our inner being, within our very own spirit.

We refuse to be like so many others who just get caught up in a bunch of doctrines about the Holy Spirit, caught up in all kinds of doctrines around your person, Holy Spirit, but we eagerly desire Your very presence, Your manifestation in our bosom, in our midst, and also amongst us when we gather together.

Father, we refuse to continue to entertain ignorance in our lives concerning spiritual things, concerning our spirit identity, and concerning the power of Your Spirit at work in us, and through us!

We refuse to water down Your gospel to mere natural information, to the mere natural realm, tickling the ears of intellectuals and philosophers and people who are sense-bound. But rather, Father, we want to break through the sense realm into the spirit realm, into the heavenly realm, into that unseen realm of spirit reality, where we walk in the Spirit, and walk by faith and not by sight, where we walk by the faith of the Son of God, and not merely our own faith, by our own opinions and beliefs.

Father, we walk in the fulfillment of Your word, and we witness with You, the confirmation of Your word ...In Jesus Name.

Paul says in Romans 10:6-8 that, *"The word is near unto you, even in your heart and in your mouth, that is the word of faith that we preach!"*

So, Father, we want to take a hold of the gospel. We want to take a hold of that faith, in our hearts. Let it also be found on our lips then, Father, because we are not going to make shipwreck of this vehicle that You give us in our spirit. Father You've given us a vehicle, called faith, and Paul says to Timothy, in 1 Timothy 1:19, that, *"some have rejected their conscience and made shipwreck of their faith"* They began in faith, *but they have neglected and then rejected the truth in their conscience.* **They no longer identified themselves with that reflection of that mirror of the word,** *and therefore they've become like an ordinary men, with ordinary faith; ordinary people, beholding their ordinary face, in an ordinary mirror:* **The world's applause; the world's opinion, the opinion of the flesh, <u>the influence and opinion of a mere natural identity</u>.**

But Father, not so with us, we are like people who are determined to look intently and deeply into the perfect law of liberty, and remain captivated by it, *until that reflection lives large within our spirits,* **so that our faith will never**

again end up shattered on the rocks because of the storms of life that come to all of us.

Father, after having now begun in faith, as we have received Jesus, as we have received the teaching concerning Him, so we are determined to walk! In Jesus name! Amen.

In closing, let me also encourage you to get yourself a copy of *"The Mirror Bible"* available on line at www.Amazon.com and several other book sellers. It is the best paraphrased version of the New Testament Scriptures, translated from the original Greek text, *that I have ever read!*

If you want me or someone who is part of our team to come to where you are, anywhere in the world, and give a talk or teach you and some of your friends about the gospel message and this magnificent work of redemption, simply contact us at www.LivingWordIntl.com, or you can always find me on Facebook.

If you have been helped, or your perspective on life has changed as a result of reading this book, or any of my many other books, please get in touch with me and let me know.

I would love to share your joy *so that my joy in writing this book may be full!*

That which was from the beginning,

which we have heard
(with our spiritual ears),
which we have seen
(with our spiritual eyes),
which we have looked upon
(beheld, focused our attention upon),
and which our hands have also handled
(which we have also experienced),

*concerning the Word of life,
we declare to you,*

*that you also may have
this fellowship with us;*

*and truly our fellowship is
with the Father
and with His Son Jesus
Christ.*

*And these things we write to you
that your joy may be full.*
— 1 John 1:1-4

About the Author

Rudi & Carmen Louw together oversee: Living Word International.

They also travel and minister both locally and internationally.

Rudi was born and raised in the country of South Africa, while Carmen grew up in Cortland, New York.

They function in the ministry of reconciliation (2 Corinthians 5:18-21) and flow strongly with the Holy Spirit and His anointing to teach, preach, prophesy, heal, and whatever is needed to touch people's lives with the reality of God's love and power.

God has given them keen insight into what He has to say to mankind, in the work of redemption, concerning the revelation and restoration of humanity's true identity.

Therefore they emphasize THE GOSPEL: IN CHRIST REALITIES, the GRACE of God, the WORD OF RIGHTEOUSNESS, *and all such eternal truths essential to salvation and living the CHRIST-LIFE.*

They have been granted this wisdom and revelation into the knowledge of God by the resurrected Spirit of Jesus Christ, *to establish and strengthen believers in the faith of God, and to activate them in ministering to others.*

Not only are people set free from the poison and bondage of sin, condemnation and all kinds of intimidation, (upheld, strengthened and reinforced by age old religious ideas, born out of ignorance) **but many are brought into a closer more intimate relationship with Father God, as Daddy**, through accurate teaching and unveiling of the gospel message, prophetic words, healings and miracles.

Rudi & Carmen are closely knitted together with many other effective Christians, church fellowships, and groups of believers who share the same revelation and passion **to transform the world we live in with the love and power of God.**

www.ingramcontent.com/pod-product-compliance
Lightning Source LLC
Chambersburg PA
CBHW071120090426
42736CB00012B/1963